Thoughts & Notions

Second Edition

Patricia Ackert | Linda Lee

THOMSON ™

HEINLE

Australia   Canada   Mexico   Singapore   United Kingdom   United States

THOMSON

HEINLE

Reading & Vocabulary Development 2: Thoughts & Notions, Second Edition
Patricia Ackert and Linda Lee

Publisher, Adult and Academic ESL:
  James W. Brown
Senior Acquisitions Editor: Sherrise Roehr
Director of Development: Anita Raducanu
Development Editor: Tom Jefferies
Editorial Assistant: Katherine Reilly
Senior Production Editor: Maryellen E. Killeen
Director of Marketing: Amy Mabley
Marketing Manager: Laura Needham
Senior Print Buyer: Mary Beth Hennebury

Compositor: Pre-Press Company, Inc.
Project Manager: Sally Lifland, Lifland et al.,
  Bookmakers
Photo Researcher: Gail Magin
Photography Manager: Sheri Blaney
Illustrator: Barry Burns
Cover Designer: Ha Ngyuen
Text Designer: Quica Ostrander
Printer: Edwards Brothers

Printed in the United States of America
1 2 3 4 5 6 7 8 9 10   07 06 05

For more information contact Heinle, 25 Thomson Place, Boston, Massachusetts 02210 USA, or you can visit out Internet site at http://www.heinle.com

For permission to use material from this text or product contact us:

Tel   1-800-730-2214
Fax   1-800-730-2215
Web   www.thomsonrights.com

ISBN: 1-413-00419-9
ISE ISBN: 1-413-00446-6

Library of Congress Control Number: TK

Contents

To the Instructor   *v*
Acknowledgments   *ix*

Unit 1   Inventions and Inventors   1

Lesson 1   The Zipper   4
Lesson 2   The Postage Stamp   9
Lesson 3   Pencils and Pens   14
Lesson 4   The Umbrella   20
Lesson 5   The Metric System   25
Word Study   31
Extension Activities
    Video Highlights: CNN Video, *An International Stamp-Making Company*   35
    Activity Page   37
    Dictionary Page: Finding Antonyms   38

Unit 2   Sports   39

Lesson 1   Thai Boxing   42
Lesson 2   Sumo Wrestling   48
Lesson 3   Tarahumara Foot Races   53
Lesson 4   Olympic Sports   59
Lesson 5   Great Athletes   64
Word Study   69
Extension Activities
    Video Highlights: CNN Video, *Scrabble®—More Than a Game*   72
    Activity Page   74
    Dictionary Page: Stress and Pronunciation   75

Unit 3   Food   77

Lesson 1   The Puffer Fish   80
Lesson 2   Foods from Around the World   85
Lesson 3   Chocolate   91
Lesson 4   The Blue Revolution   97
Lesson 5   Twenty-One Days Without Food   103

Word Study   108
Extension Activities
      Video Highlights: CNN Video, *The Puffer Fish—*
         A Gourmet Japanese Food   112
      Activity Page   114
      Dictionary Page: Parts of Speech   115

? Unit 4   Mysteries   117

Lesson 1   The Marie Celeste   120
Lesson 2   The Roanoke Settlement   126
Lesson 3   The Easter Island Statues   132
Lesson 4   The Tunguska Fireball   138
Lesson 5   Mystery of the Monarchs   144
Word Study   150
Extension Activities
      Video Highlights: CNN Video, *Modern-Day Easter Island*   155
      Activity Page   157
      Dictionary Page: Informal Usage   159

Unit 5   Business   161

Lesson 1   The History of Money   164
Lesson 2   Mass Marketing   171
Lesson 3   Inflation   177
Lesson 4   Doing Business Around the World   184
Lesson 5   Plastic Money   192
Word Study   198
Extension Activities
      Video Highlights: CNN Video, *Coca Cola®—*
         An International Organization   203
      Activity Page   206
      Dictionary Page: Capitalization and Abbreviation   207

Vocabulary   209
Skills Index   212
Irregular Verbs   214

To the Instructor

Reading & Vocabulary Development 2: Thoughts & Notions is a best-selling beginning reading skills text designed for students of English as a second or foreign language who have a basic vocabulary in English of about 800 words. This text teaches about 500 more words. It also teaches the reading skills of comprehension, finding the main idea, and using the context to understand vocabulary items.

Thoughts & Notions is one in a series of reading skills texts. The complete series has been designed to meet the needs of students from the beginning to the high intermediate levels and includes the following:

Reading & Vocabulary Development 1: Facts & Figures
Reading & Vocabulary Development 2: Thoughts & Notions
Reading & Vocabulary Development 3: Cause & Effect
Reading & Vocabulary Development 4: Concepts & Comments

In addition to the student text, an answer key and video transcript, VHS, DVD, audio cassette, and audio CD are also available for *Thoughts & Notions*. *Thoughts & Notions* uses the following methodology:

• **Theme-based approach to reading.** Each of the five units has a theme such as sports, food, or business.

• **Systematic presentation and recycling of vocabulary.** One of the primary tasks of beginning students is developing a useful and personally relevant vocabulary base. In *Thoughts & Notions*, up to twelve words are introduced in each lesson. These words appear in boldface type. Those underlined are illustrated or glossed in the margin. All of the new vocabulary items are used several times in the lesson, and then are systematically recycled throughout the text.

• **Pedagogical design.** The central goal of *Thoughts & Notions* is to help students develop the critical reading skills they will need for academic, personal, and/or career purposes. Toward this end, each unit offers a comprehensive program that begins with pre-reading questions, continues with reading and discussion, and proceeds through a set of carefully sequenced post-reading activities.

Organization of *Thoughts & Notions*

Thoughts & Notions is organized into five units. Each unit contains five lessons packed with exercises and activities.

- **Context Clues.** A context clue exercise at the beginning of each unit introduces some of the vocabulary for the following unit. This section is designed to pre-teach particularly important vocabulary items.

- **"Before You Read" Questions.** These pre-reading questions provide a motivation for reading the text.

- **Vocabulary.** The first exercise has sentences taken directly from the text. All new words are included. This is for practice in reading the sentences again and writing the new words.

- **Vocabulary: New Context.** This exercise gives further practice with the new words in a different context but with the same meaning.

- **Vocabulary Review.** Vocabulary items are used in subsequent texts and exercises to give additional review. They are fill-ins or matching synonyms and antonyms.

- **Comprehension.** These exercises are true/false, true/false/ no information, or multiple choice. They include inference and discussion questions marked with an asterisk.

- **Questions.** These comprehension questions are taken directly from the text. Those marked with an asterisk are either inference or discussion questions.

- **Main Idea.** Students must choose the main idea of the text from three possibilities.

- **Word Study.** A word study section is provided near the end of each unit. It reinforces structural points, such as verb forms,

vi

pronouns, and comparison of adjectives, that the students are learning in other classes. It also gives spelling rules for noun plurals and verb endings. Later units have charts of word forms. The exercises are not intended to be complete explanations and practice of the grammar points.

- **Writing.** Each word study section closes with a writing exercise.

- **Extension Activities.** Each unit ends with a set of high-interest, interactive tasks to help students practice the new vocabulary and the skills they have learned in more open-ended contexts.

CNN Video Highlights—The highlight of each set of extension activities is a short video-based lesson centered on a stimulating, authentic clip from the CNN video archives. Each video lesson follows the same sequence of activities:

Before You Watch encourages students to recall background knowledge based on their own experiences or from information presented in the readings.

As You Watch asks students to watch for general information such as the topic of the clip.

After You Watch gets the students to expand on the main points of the video by establishing further connections to the reading passages, their own experiences, and their ideas and opinions.

Activity Page—Games found on this page encourage students to practice the vocabulary and structures found in that unit's lessons in a relaxed, open-ended way.

Dictionary Page—Exercises on this page offer students practice with dictionary skills based on entries from *The Basic Newbury House Dictionary.*

- **Skills Index.** This index provides teachers and students with a handy reference for all of the reading and writing skills introduced in *Thoughts & Notions,* as well as all of the grammatical structures found in the text.

New to This Edition

The best-selling reading series just got better! The second edition of *Thoughts & Notions* contains new readings, new pedagogy, and new ancillaries.

• Six fresh new readings engage students in fascinating new topics. The new readings for this edition are as follows:

Unit 2, Lesson 4: Olympic Sports
Unit 2, Lesson 5: Great Athletes
Unit 3, Lesson 4: The Blue Revolution
Unit 3, Lesson 5: Twenty-One Days Without Food
Unit 4, Lesson 5: Mystery of the Monarchs
Unit 5, Lesson 5: Plastic Money

• Thoroughly checked for factual accuracy, each reading has been revised to include level-appropriate structures and vocabulary.

• New collocation activities throughout the text help students understand how words fit together in chunks.

• New pedagogical design, photos, and illustrations aid student comprehension and ease navigation through the text.

• *ExamView® Pro* test-generating software allows instructors to create custom tests and quizzes.

• A new website (found at <u>http://elt.thomson.com/readingandvocabulary</u>) features vocabulary flashcards, crossword puzzles, quizzes, and more to help students review for tests.

Acknowledgments

The authors and publisher would like to thank the following individuals who offered helpful feedback and suggestions for the revision of the *Reading & Vocabulary Development* series:

Brian Altano—Bergen Community College, Paramus, NJ

Benjamin Deleon—Delano High School, Delano, CA

Elaine Dow—Quinsigamond Community College, Worcester, MA

Julia Karet—Chaffey College, Rancho Cucamonga, CA

Jane Sitko—Edmonds Community College, Lynnwood, WA

Inventions and Inventors

Context Clues

Put a circle around the letter of the answer that means the same as the word in bold.

1. The two brothers lived together in New York for several years. Then one of them moved to California. Now they are living **apart.**
   a. above each other
   b. beside each other
   c. not together
   d. near each other

2. Ali keeps a **strip** of paper in his book so he can remember what page he is on.
   a. heavy piece
   b. dark piece
   c. long, thin piece
   d. dirty piece

3. There is a **row** of trees along each side of our street.
   a. line
   b. forest
   c. record
   d. piece

4. Half a **dozen** eggs is six eggs.
   a. fourteen
   b. twelve
   c. eight
   d. sixteen

5. Someone **delivers** a newspaper to my apartment every morning. I don't have to go out and buy one.
   a. uses
   b. brings
   c. destroys
   d. connects

6. I tried to pay for their help, but they wouldn't **accept** my money.
   a. bring
   b. shoot
   c. take
   d. suppose

7. Sara **received** a package from her parents yesterday. They sent her some new clothes.
   a. needed
   b. got
   c. spent
   d. told

8. Stop talking **immediately!** The test started five minutes ago.
   a. today   c. later
   b. soon   d. right now

9. I don't have to work or go to class today. I can do **whatever** I want to do.
   a. anything   c. anytime
   b. anywhere   d. anyone

10. Saudi Arabia has a desert **climate.** Canada has a cold **climate** in winter. The **climate** in Indonesia is tropical.
    a. type of land   c. government
    b. average weather   d. food

lesson

1

The Zipper

© Michael Newman/Photo Edit

Before You Read

1. Are you wearing something with a zipper?

2. What can you do when a zipper on a piece of clothing breaks?

3. Do you have any clothing without a zipper? How does it close?

1   The Zipper

The **zipper** is a wonderful invention. How did people ever live without zippers? They are very common, so we forget that they are wonderful. They are very strong, but they open and close very easily. They come in many colors and sizes.

In the 1890s, people in the United States wore high shoes with a long **row** of buttons. Clothes often had rows of buttons, too. People wished that clothes were easier to put on and take off.

line

Whitcomb L. Judson, an **engineer** from the United States, invented the zipper in 1893. However, his zippers didn't stay closed very well. This was **embarrassing,** and people didn't buy many of them. Then Dr. Gideon Sundback from Sweden **solved** this problem. His zipper stayed closed.

A zipper has three parts: 1. There are **dozens** of metal or plastic **hooks** (called *teeth*) in two rows. 2. These hooks are **fastened** to two **strips** of cloth. The cloth strips are flexible. They **bend** easily. 3. A fastener **slides** along and joins the hooks together. When it slides the other way, it takes the hooks **apart.**

a dozen = 12

joined or attached

Dr. Sundback put the hooks on strips of cloth. The cloth holds all the hooks in place. They don't come apart very easily. This solved the problem of the first zippers.

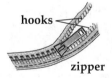

hooks

zipper

a Vocabulary

Put the right word in each blank. The sentences are from the text.

zipper	embarrassing	hooks	dozens
solved	bend	fastened	apart
strips	row	engineer	slides

1. In the 1890s, people in the United States wore high shoes with a long _____ of buttons.

2. There are _____ of metal or plastic _____ (called *teeth*) in two rows.

3. The _____ is a wonderful invention.

4. A fastener _____ along and joins the hooks together.

5. Whitcomb L. Judson, an _____ from the United States, invented the zipper in 1893.

6. When it slides the other way, it takes the hooks _____.

7. This was _____, and people didn't buy many of them.

8. They _____ easily.

9. These hooks are _____ to two _____ of cloth.

10. Then Dr. Gideon Sundback from Sweden _____ this problem.

b Vocabulary: New Context

Put the right word in each blank.

fasteners	engineer	zippers	slide
apart	hook	dozen	strips
solve	bend	embarrassed	rows

1. Icy roads are dangerous because cars _____ on them.

2. Pam cut a piece of paper into five _____.

3. Sometimes your face gets red when you feel _____.

4. Do you like to _____ math problems?

5. You can catch fish with a _____.

6. Hooks, buttons, and zippers are all _____.

7. American supermarkets sell eggs by the _____.

8. Tony and George had an apartment together, but now they live _____.

9. Students sit in a circle in some classes. They sit in _____ in others.

10. You _____ your knees when you sit down.

11. Most pants and jackets have _____.

12. An _____ knows how to build a road.

C   Comprehension

Put a circle around the letter of the best answer.

1. Zippers open and close by _____.
   a. shooting   c. bending
   b. sliding   d. choosing

2. The hooks on a zipper are _____.
   a. plastic   c. cloth
   b. metal   d. a or b

3. Mr. Judson was an _____.
   a. engineer   c. American
   b. inventor   d. a, b, and c

4. Mr. Judson didn't sell many zippers because _____.
   a. they were hard to open and close
   b. people liked rows of buttons
   c. they came open very easily
   d. they had cloth strips

5. Dr. Sundback was _____.
   a. a Swede   c. an American
   b. from Chicago   d. a professor

6. A zipper has two _____ of cloth.
   a. rows   c. strips
   b. fasteners   d. buttons

7. The _____ on a zipper are flexible.
   a. hooks   c. fasteners
   b. rows of buttons   d. strips of cloth

8. Dr. Sundback _____.
   a. invented the zipper   c. invented the button hook
   b. made the zipper better   d. sold high shoes

 d Questions

The asterisk (*) means you have to think of the answer. You cannot find it in the text.

1. Why do we forget that zippers are wonderful?
2. Are zippers strong?
3. What kind of shoes did Americans wear in the 1890s?
4. Who invented the zipper? When did he invent it?
5. Why were the first zippers embarrassing?
6. What country was Dr. Sundback from?
7. Describe a zipper. How does it work?
8. What part of the zipper is flexible?
9. What did Dr. Sundback do to make zippers better?
*10. What is a newer kind of fastener than the zipper?

 e Main Idea

Which is the main idea of this lesson? Choose one.

1. A zipper has hooks, cloth strips, and a slide fastener.
2. People didn't like the first zippers.
3. Mr. Judson and Dr. Sundback gave us a wonderful invention, the zipper.

lesson 2

The Postage Stamp

Before You Read

1. Does someone in the class have a postage stamp? What does it look like?

2. How much does it cost to mail a letter today?

3. Name a famous person on a postage stamp.

2 The Postage Stamp

Before the invention of the **postage stamp,** it was difficult to send a letter to another country. The sender paid for the letter to travel in his or her own country. Then the person in the other country paid for the rest of the trip. If a letter **crossed** several countries, the problem was worse.

went from one side to the other

Rowland Hill, a British teacher, had the idea of a postage stamp with **glue** on the back. The British post office made the first stamps in 1840. They were the Penny Black and the Twopence Blue. A person bought a stamp and put it on a letter. The post office **delivered** the letter. When people **received** letters, they didn't have to pay anything. The postage was **prepaid.**

took to a person or place

got

paid for in advance

Postage stamps became popular in Great Britain **immediately.** Other countries started making their own postage stamps very quickly.

right away, right now

There were still problems with international **mail.** Some countries did not want to **accept** letters with stamps from other countries. Finally, in 1874, a German organized the Universal Postal Union (UPU). Each country in the UPU agreed to accept letters with prepaid postage from the other **members.** Today, the offices of the UPU are in Switzerland. Almost every country in the world is a member of this organization. It takes care of any international mail problems.

take

Today, post offices in every country sell beautiful stamps. Collecting stamps is one of the most popular hobbies in the world, and every stamp collector knows about the Penny Black and the Twopence Blue.

a Vocabulary

Put the right word in each blank. The sentences are from the text.

crossed	received	postage	mail
prepaid	members	immediately	accept
stamp	delivered	glue	

1. When people _____ letters, they didn't have to pay anything.

2. Before the invention of the _____ _____, it was difficult to send a letter to another country.

3. The post office _____ the letter.

4. Each country in the UPU agreed to accept letters with prepaid postage from the other _____.

5. If a letter _____ several countries, the problem was worse.

6. Postage stamps became popular in Great Britain _____.

7. Some countries did not want to _____ letters with stamps from other countries.

8. The postage was _____.

9. There were still problems with international _____.

10. Rowland Hill, a British teacher, had the idea of a postage stamp with _____ on the back.

b Vocabulary: New Context

Put the right word in each blank.

prepay	cross	postage	members
deliver	mail	immediately	receive
accept	stamps	glue	

1. Jamal and Marie are _____ of the International Students Club.

2. When you rent an apartment for a year, you have to _____ the last month's rent.

3. Children have to be careful when they _____ the street.

4. Mr. Ross is going to the post office because he has to buy some
   _____ .

5. If you buy furniture, the store will _____ it to your house.

6. How much is the _____ for an airmail letter to Japan?

7. Did you _____ any letters this week?

8. Please go to your office _____ . You have a long-distance phone call.

9. The teacher will not _____ homework if it is late. You must do it on time.

10. Did you get any _____ today?

11. _____ helps a stamp stay on a letter.

c Comprehension: True/False/No Information

Write T if the sentence is true. Write F if it is false. Write NI if no information about the sentence was given in the text.

_____ 1. Before postage stamps, two people paid for letters that went from one country to another.

_____ 2. A teacher invented the postage stamp.

_____ 3. The inventor of the postage stamp was American.

_____ 4. The first two stamps were colored black and blue.

_____ 5. A stamp shows that the postage is prepaid.

_____ 6. The United States was the second country to make postage stamps.

_____ 7. Postage stamps solved all mail problems immediately.

_____ 8. Members of the UPU accept prepaid letters from other countries.

_____ 9. Kuwait is a member of the UPU.

_____10. All the UPU officials are Swiss.

_____11. Stamp collecting is a popular hobby.

 d Questions

The asterisk (*) means you have to think of the answer. You cannot find it in the text.

1. Why was it difficult to send a letter to another country before the invention of the postage stamp?
2. Who invented the postage stamp?
3. When did he invent it?
4. What country was he from?
5. Did it take long for postage stamps to become popular?
*6. Why were they popular?
7. What does _prepaid_ mean?
*8. Why didn't countries want to accept mail with stamps from other countries?
9. What does the Universal Postal Union do today?
10. Where are its offices?
11. Why do people like to collect stamps?
12. Why do stamp collectors know about the Penny Black?

 e Main Idea

Which is the main idea of this lesson? Choose one.

1. Rowland Hill, a British teacher, invented the postage stamp.
2. When Mr. Hill invented the postage stamp, it solved a big problem.
3. People collect stamps because every country makes beautiful ones.

Pencils and Pens

lesson

3

© Jim Franco/Taxi/getty images

Before You Read

1. Do you usually do your homework in pen or in pencil? Why?

2. Which is more useful—a pencil or a pen? Why do you think so?

3. How do people sharpen pencils?

14

3   Pencils and Pens

No one knows who invented pencils or when it happened. A Swiss described a pencil in a book in 1565. He said it was a piece of wood with **lead** inside it. (Lead is a very heavy, soft, dark gray metal.) Pencils weren't popular, and people continued to write with pens. They used bird feathers as pens.

Then, in 1795, someone started making pencils from **graphite,** and they became very popular. Graphite is like coal. (Coal is black, and we burn it for heat and energy.) Today, people make pencils in the same way. They **grind** the graphite, make it into the **shape** of a stick, and bake it. Then they put it inside a piece of wood. One pencil can write 50,000 English words or make a line 55 kilometers long.

People wrote with feather pens and then used pens with metal **points.** They had to **dip** the point into **ink** after every few letters. Next, someone invented a **fountain pen** that could **hold** ink inside it. A fountain pen can write several pages before you have to **fill** it again.

fountain pen

Two Hungarian brothers, Ladislao and Georg Biro, invented the **ballpoint pen.** They left Hungary and started making ballpoint pens in England in 1943, during World War II. English pilots liked the pens. They couldn't write with fountain pens in airplanes because the ink **leaked** out. Later, a French company called Bic bought the Biros' company.

ballpoint pen

Some people call ballpoint pens "Bics." Australians call them "biros." **Whatever** we call them, we use them every day.

leak

anything

a Vocabulary

Put the right word in each blank. The sentences are from the text.

ballpoint pen	points	lead	leaked	graphite
shape	grind	dip	whatever	
hold	ink	fill	fountain pen	

1. They couldn't write with fountain pens in airplanes because the ink
   _____ out.

2. A fountain pen can write several pages before you have to
   _____ it again.

3. He said it was a piece of wood with _____ inside it.

4. People wrote with feather pens and then used pens with metal
   _____.

5. Next someone invented a _____ that could
   _____ ink inside it.

6. They had to _____ the point into _____ after
   every few letters.

7. They _____ the graphite, make it into the
   _____ of a stick, and bake it.

8. Two Hungarian brothers, Ladislao and Georg Biro, invented the
   _____.

9. _____ we call them, we use them every day.

10. Then, in 1795, someone started making pencils from _____,
    and they became very popular.

b Vocabulary: New Context

Put the right word in each blank.

ballpoint pens	shape	lead	holds	graphite
ink	leaks	grind	fill	
point	dipped	whatever	fountain pen	

1. Our shower _____. A little water runs out of it all day.

2. A bathtub _____ a lot of water.

3. You should have a good _____ on your pencil.
4. I hope they _____ the hole in the road soon. It's dangerous.
5. The sun has the _____ of a circle.
6. Students a hundred years ago always had a bottle of _____ on their desks.
7. She _____ her fingers in the water to see if it was cold.
8. We _____ coffee before we mix it with hot water.
9. Most people use _____, but some people prefer fountain pens.
10. At a cafeteria, you can choose _____ you want to eat.
11. Pencils are still made with _____.
12. Elena filled her new _____ with purple ink.

C   Vocabulary Review

Put the right word in each blank.

apart	slide	embarrassed	immediately
bend	row	member	
dozen	hook	stamp	

1. There are about a _____ students in the class. It is a small class.
2. If you want to be on time, you should leave _____.
3. Are you a _____ of any clubs or organizations?
4. People often _____ over when they talk to children.
5. A children's park usually has a _____ and a swing.
6. Masako was _____ when she gave the wrong answer in class.
7. Robert took his bicycle _____, and now he can't put it back together again.
8. There is a _____ on the back of the door. You can hang your coat on it.
9. Maria always sits in the front _____ of the class.
10. Jay put a _____ on the letter and mailed it at the post office.

d Comprehension: Multiple Choice

Put a circle around the letter of the best answer. The asterisk (*) means you have to think of the answer. You cannot find it in the text.

1. A _____ described a pencil in 1565.
   - a. Hungarian
   - b. Swiss
   - c. Swede
   - d. German

2. The first pencils had _____ in them.
   - a. gold
   - b. graphite
   - c. lead
   - d. ink

3. One pencil can write _____ English words.
   - a. 50,000
   - b. 55,000
   - c. 55
   - d. 1565

4. The first pens were _____.
   - a. wooden
   - b. stone
   - c. feathers
   - d. graphite

5. The next pens had a _____ point.
   - a. wooden
   - b. lead
   - c. metal
   - d. silver

6. A fountain pen can hold _____ inside it.
   - a. coal
   - b. lead
   - c. graphite
   - d. ink

7. The Biro brothers made thousands of pens in _____.
   - a. England
   - b. Hungary
   - c. France
   - d. Switzerland

8. _____ are best for writing in airplanes.
   - a. Ballpoint pens
   - b. Pencils
   - c. Fountain pens
   - d. a and b

*9. People burn _____.
   - a. coal and graphite
   - b. graphite and lead
   - c. coal and wood
   - d. lead and coal

*10. People grind _____.
   - a. hamburger meat
   - b. coffee
   - c. graphite
   - d. a, b, and c

 Questions

The asterisk (*) means you have to think of the answer. You cannot find it in the text.

1. Describe the pencils in 1565.
2. Describe a modern pencil.
3. How do people make pencils today?
4. What kind of pens did people write with after feather pens?
5. Why was a fountain pen better than the old pens?
6. Who invented the ballpoint pen?
7. Where were the inventors of the ballpoint pen from?
8. Why is a ballpoint pen better than a fountain pen for a pilot?
*9. Why does a fountain pen leak in an airplane?
10. In what country were Bic pens first made?
11. Where did the word *biro* come from?
*12. Which is better—a pencil or a ballpoint pen?

Main Idea

Which is the main idea of this lesson? Choose one.

1. There were several kinds of pens before ballpoint pens.
2. We use pens and pencils every day.
3. Ballpoint pens and pencils are very useful inventions.

The Umbrella

© Benelux Press/Index Stock Imagery

Before You Read

1. Do you have an umbrella? How often do you use it?

2. What do you do when it rains and you do not have an umbrella?

3. Some people say that you shouldn't open an umbrella inside a house. They say it is bad luck. Do you believe this?

4   The Umbrella

The umbrella is a very ordinary **object.** It keeps the rain and the sun off people. Most umbrellas **fold up,** so it is easy to carry them.

thing

However, the umbrella has not always been an ordinary object. In the past, it was a sign of **royalty** or importance. Some African **tribes** still use umbrellas in this way. Someone carries an umbrella and walks behind the king or important person.

kings, queens, and their families

Umbrellas are very old. The Chinese had them more than 3,000 years ago. From there, umbrellas traveled to India, Persia, and Egypt. In Greece and Rome, men **wouldn't** use them. They believed umbrellas were only for women.

past of *won't*

When the Spanish explorers went to Mexico, they saw the Aztec kings using umbrellas. English explorers saw Native American **princes** carrying umbrellas on the east coast of North America. It **seems** that people in different parts of the world invented umbrellas at different times.

sons of kings and queens

England was probably the first country in Europe where ordinary people used umbrellas against the rain. England has a rainy **climate,** and umbrellas are very useful there.

Everybody uses umbrellas today. The next time you carry one, remember that for centuries only great men and women used them. Perhaps you are really a king or queen, a **princess** or prince.

daughter of a king and queen

21

a   Vocabulary

Put the right word in each blank. The sentences are from the text.

wouldn't	princes	tribes
object	climate	fold up
royalty	princes	seems

1. English explorers saw Native American _____ carrying umbrellas on the east coast of North America.
2. In the past, it was a sign of _____ or importance.
3. England has a rainy _____, and umbrellas are very useful there.
4. The umbrella is a very ordinary _____.
5. In Greece and Rome, men _____ use them.
6. Perhaps you are really a king or queen, a _____ or prince.
7. Some African _____ still use umbrellas in this way.
8. Most umbrellas _____, so it is easy to carry them.
9. It _____ that people in different parts of the world invented umbrellas at different times.

b   Vocabulary: New Context

Put the right word in each blank.

prince	princess	objects
folded up	wouldn't	climate
royalty	tribe	seems

1. A _____ is the daughter of a king and queen. A _____ is the son of a king and queen. They are all _____.
2. Bill _____ very unhappy today. What is wrong?
3. The Yanomami had no metal. They only had _____ made of wood and stone.
4. Dan asked Maria to go to the movies with him last night, but she _____ go. She was too tired.

5. The Hopi are a _____ in Arizona.

6. Qatar has a desert _____, but Malaysia has a tropical one.

7. He _____ the letter and put it in an envelope.

C Vocabulary Review

Match the word in Column A with the word in Column B that means the opposite. The first one is done for you.

Column A

1. apart   *e. together*
2. ordinary   _____
3. receive   _____
4. accept   _____
5. fill   _____
6. fasten   _____
7. solve   _____
8. hold   _____
9. immediately   _____

Column B

a. empty
b. cause
c. later
d. uncommon
e. together
f. let go
g. take apart
h. refuse
i. send

d Comprehension: Multiple Choice

Put a circle around the letter of the best answer.

1. Today, people use umbrellas for _____.
   a. the rain
   b. the sun
   c. a sign of a great person
   d. a, b, and c

2. A queen is a _____ person.
   a. royal
   b. embarrassing
   c. holiday
   d. jewelry

3. A great person walks _____ someone with an umbrella.
   a. beside
   b. next to
   c. in front of
   d. in back of

4. India and Persia learned about umbrellas from _____.
   a. Aztecs
   b. Egypt
   c. China
   d. Spanish explorers

5. Most nations had some kind of _____ in the past.
   a. coal   c. ink
   b. royalty   d. mail delivery

6. Native Americans _____.
   a. learned about umbrellas from English and Spanish explorers
   b. invented umbrellas
   c. got umbrellas from the Chinese
   d. taught the English about umbrellas

7. English people started using umbrellas because they have _____.
   a. royalty   c. too much sun
   b. a rainy climate   d. many great men and women

 Questions

The asterisk (*) means you have to think of the answer. You cannot find it in the text.

1. What are two uses of an umbrella?
*2. Why is it easier to carry an umbrella that folds up?
3. What was an umbrella a sign of in the past?
4. Who uses umbrellas in this way today?
*5. How do we know that the Chinese had umbrellas over 3,000 years ago?
6. Why didn't Greek men use umbrellas?
7. What other people invented the umbrella?
8. Why did English people like umbrellas?
*9. In what countries are umbrellas not very useful?

 Main Idea

Which is the main idea for this lesson? Choose one.

1. For centuries, only great people used umbrellas; now, ordinary people everywhere use them.
2. Umbrellas are useful in the rain.
3. The Chinese and the Native Americans invented umbrellas.

24

The Metric System

lesson

5

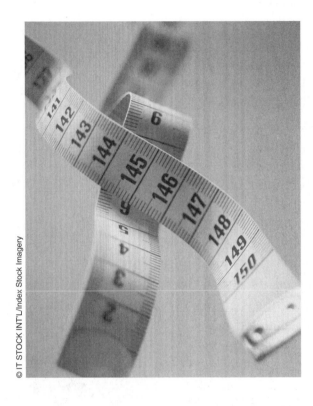

© IT STOCK INT'L/Index Stock Imagery

METRIC MEASURES
Length
1 millimeter [mm]
1 centimeter [cm] = 10 mm
1 meter [m] = 100 cm
1 kilometer [km] = 1,000 m

Volume
1 milliliter [mL]
1 centiliter [cL] = 100 mL
1 liter [L] = 100 cL
1 kiloliter [kL] = 1,000 L

Weight
1 milligram [mg]
1 gram [g] = 1,000 mg
1 kilogram [kg] = 1,000 g
1 metric ton [t] = 1,000 kg

Before You Read

1. Does your country use the metric system?

2. Do you know another system of measurement?

3. Which countries do not use the metric system?

5   The Metric System

People all over the world use grams, kilograms (kilos), meters, and liters. These are all ways to **measure** things. They are all part of the **metric system.**

During the French **Revolution** (1789–1799) against the king, the revolutionary government started the metric system. Before that, every part of France had a different system for measuring things. Also, cloth makers measured cloth with one system. Jewelers used another system. **Carpenters** used another. Other countries used different systems. The revolutionary government wanted one scientific system of measurement. They asked a group of scientists and mathematicians to invent a system.

The mathematicians and scientists **decided** to use the numbers ten, hundred, and thousand for their system.

Next, they had to decide on a "natural" **length.** They chose one ten-millionth (1/10,000,000) of the **distance** from the **equator** to the North Pole. They called this distance the meter. Then they chose the gram for weighing things. A **cubic** centimeter of water weighs 1 gram.

Mathematicians and scientists worked for 20 years until they finally had a complete measuring system. The biggest problem was measuring the meter.

The metric system was a wonderful gift to the world. There are only a few countries that don't use it. The United States is one. The metric system is truly an international system.

war by people against their government

people who build things with wood

noun for *long*

how far it is between two places

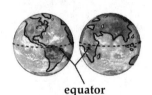

equator

cube
(adjective = cubic)

a Vocabulary

Put the right word in each blank. The sentences are from the text.

| Revolution | equator | cubic | length | carpenters |
| system | metric | measure | distance | decided |

1. During the French _____ (1789–1799) against the king, the revolutionary government started the metric system.
2. Next, they had to decide on a "natural" _____.
3. They are all part of the _____ _____.
4. A _____ centimeter of water weighs 1 gram.
5. They chose one ten-millionth (1/10,000,000) of the _____ from the _____ to the North Pole.
6. These are all ways to _____ things.
7. Also, cloth makers measured cloth with one system. Jewelers used another system. _____ used another.
8. The mathematicians and scientists _____ to use the numbers ten, hundred, and thousand for their system.

b Vocabulary: New Context

Put the right word in each blank.

| distance | system | equator | metric | cube |
| carpenter | Revolution | measure | length | |

1. The Russian _____ in 1917 was against the royal family of Russia.
2. What is the _____ between Chicago and New York?
3. The _____ system is a system of measurement.
4. A _____ added a new room to our house.
5. We need to buy a tablecloth. Please _____ the table so we will know what size to buy. What is the _____ of the table?
6. Indonesia, Kenya, and the Amazon River are all near the _____.
7. A _____ has six sides. Each side is the same size.
8. The British had the first _____ of prepaid postage.

c Vocabulary Review

Put the right word in each blank.

postage	crossed	fill	whatever
immediately	deliver	dipped	length
member	point	hold	distance

1. Fifty years ago, it took a long time to get the news. Now you can get it _____.

2. Do you want me to _____ that old pen with ink?

3. I am happy to do _____ you want to do.

4. Letters that go outside a country need more _____ than letters inside a country.

5. How many pencils can you _____ in one hand?

6. Did the mail carrier _____ the mail yet?

7. The _____ on my pencil is broken. May I sharpen it?

8. What is the _____ between San Francisco and Los Angeles?

9. She _____ her fingers in the water to see if it was cold.

10. My new pants are the wrong _____. I need to shorten them.

11. The Polynesians _____ the Pacific Ocean in double canoes.

12. Carl is a _____ of the stamp club. Collecting stamps is his hobby.

d Comprehension: True/False/No Information

Write T if the sentence is true. Write F if it is false. Write NI if no information about the sentence was given in the text.

_____ 1. The kilogram is part of the metric system.

_____ 2. Hectares are part of the metric system.

_____ 3. We use the metric system to measure things.

_____ 4. The French Revolution was in the 17th century.

_____ 5. The metric system is an international scientific system of measurement.

_____ 6. Mathematicians and scientists invented the metric system.

_____ 7. France gave the world a wonderful gift—the metric system.

_____ 8. The United States uses the metric system.

_____ 9. The United States uses an old English system of measurement.

_____ 10. The French Revolution happened after the American Revolution.

e | Questions

The asterisk (*) means you have to think of the answer. You cannot find it in the text.

  *1. What do *centi-* and *milli-* mean?
  2. What is the metric system?
  3. Who was the French Revolution against?
  4. Before the Revolution, the French people had a problem about measuring things. What was it?
  5. Who invented the metric system?
  6. What did they choose for the "natural" length?
  7. How did they measure a gram?
  8. How long did it take to complete the metric system?
  9. Why is this system of measurement called "international"?
*10. Why is the metric system easy to use?

f Main Idea

Match the inventions and the details. Write the number of the invention on the line before the detail. The first one is done for you. Some details go with more than one invention.

Inventions

1. the zipper
2. the postage stamp
3. the pencil
4. the ballpoint pen
5. the umbrella
6. the metric system

Details

_2_ a. A British teacher invented it.

_____ b. French scientists and mathematicians invented it.

_____ c. Different groups of people invented it.

_____ d. An American invented it.

_____ e. No one knows who invented it.

_____ f. Two Hungarian brothers invented it.

_____ g. It is international and scientific.

_____ h. Sometimes it is a sign of royalty.

_____ i. The United States doesn't use it.

_____ j. It is a fastener.

_____ k. It can write 50,000 English words.

_____ l. It works better than a fountain pen in an airplane.

_____ m. People in many countries use it.

_____ n. Collecting them is a popular hobby.

Word Study

a   *Will* or *be + going to*

There are two ways to write about the future in English. You can use *will* or a form of *be* with *going to*.

* *Will* + simple verb

    Examples: Carol **will lend** me her car tomorrow.

                    Classes **will end** next week.

* *Be* (*am, is,* or *are*) + *going to* + simple verb

    Examples: The store **is going to deliver** our new refrigerator this afternoon.

                    I **am going to measure** the kitchen floor.

1. *Write sentences with* will, *the verb given, and the word or words in parentheses.*

    Example: travel (next summer)
    My parents will travel in Japan for two months next summer.

    a. receive (next week)
    b. deliver (tomorrow)
    c. decide (tonight)
    d. arrive (tomorrow morning)
    e. go skiing (next winter)

2. *Write sentences with* be (am, is, *or* are) going to, *the verb given, and the word or words in parentheses.*

    Example: attend (next week)
    I am going to attend my cousin's wedding next week.

    a. continue (next fall)
    b. practice (all summer)
    c. choose (next week)
    d. mail (tomorrow)
    e. leave (next month)

31

b How + adjective

Examples: **How far** is it to Los Angeles? **How old** are you?
How large is your country? **How heavy** is a hippopotamus?

Use these words in questions.

1. how long
2. how deep
3. how tall
4. how much
5. how fast

c Irregular Verbs

1. *Learn these verb forms. Then use each past form in a sentence.*

Simple	Past
a. keep	kept
b. hurt	hurt
c. lead	led
d. write	wrote
e. wear	wore
f. freeze	froze
g. lose	lost
h. pay	paid
i. speak	spoke
j. build	built

2. *Write the past form of each verb.*

a. blow _____
b. give _____
c. know _____
d. shop _____
e. meet _____
f. understand _____

g. choose _____
h. grow _____
i. leave _____
j. send _____
k. fall _____

d Word Forms

	Verb	Noun	Adjective
1.	collect	collection, collector	collectable
2.	describe	description	descriptive
3.	heat	heat	hot
4.	(none)	royalty	royal
5.	(none)	importance	important
6.	pollute	pollution	polluted
7.	believe	belief	believable
8.	rain	rain	rainy
9.	sharpen	sharpener	sharp
10.	measure	measurement	measurable

Put the correct word form in each blank. Use words from line 1 above for item 1, and so on. Use the right form of the verb and singular or plural nouns.

1. Lois is a stamp _____. She _____ stamps.

2. Write a _____ of your city. _____ your city to your classmates.

3. We need some _____ water. Please _____ some.

4. Prince Charles is a member of the British _____ family. His parents are _____, too.

5. In India, umbrellas were a sign of _____. Only _____ people used them.

6. Toxic substances are a form of _____. They can _____ the air and the water. Then the environment is _____.

7. Many people _____ that the oceans are dying.

8. It is starting to _____. We are going to have a _____ day. Do you like the _____?

9. Where is the pencil _____? My pencil isn't _____. I need to _____ it.

10. Please _____ the size of the living room carpet. How long and how wide is it? What are the _____?

 Writing

Choose one or more of these topics and write answers.

1. Which inventions in Unit 1 are the most important in your own life? Why?
2. What do you want someone to invent? Describe it.
3. Think of another important invention. Describe it.

Video Highlights

a Before You Watch

1. What do you know about the famous people in this chart? Work with a small group to fill in the rest of the chart. You do not need to use complete sentences.

Famous People	Facts about Them
Elvis Presley	*Rock-and-roll singer, lived in the United States*
Marilyn Monroe	
Ronald Reagan	
Sylvester Stallone	
John Lennon	
Barbara Streisand	
Pope John Paul	

2. Have you seen these people on stamps? What other famous people have you seen on stamps?

b As You Watch

Check the countries whose names you hear in the video.

☐ Canada
☐ Uganda
☐ Switzerland
☐ China
☐ the United States
☐ Mexico

☐ Grenada
☐ Honduras
☐ Cameroon
☐ Liberia
☐ Ghana
☐ St. Vincent and the Grenadines

C   After You Watch

1. *Look at the map and find two of the countries from the list on the previous page. Circle the countries.*

2. *Read the information about the postal system in one of these countries, and answer the questions that follow.*

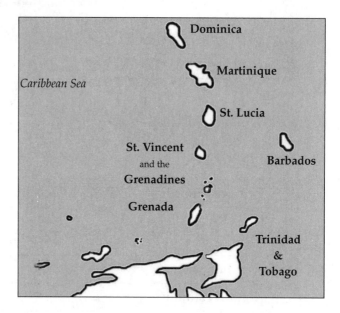

Grenada is a small island in the Caribbean Sea. Its population is about 104,000, and its official language is English. Grenada is a member of the Universal Postal Union, so Grenadians can send and receive international mail. However, no one in the country has the equipment necessary to produce stamps.

The Philatela Company in New York City produces stamps for more than seventy countries. Like Grenada, most of these countries do not make their own stamps. They must buy them from another place. Many of the stamps that the Grenadian postal system buys from Philatela have beautiful pictures of famous people on them. The company artists design the stamps, and the post office officials decide if they like them or not. Sometimes, new stamps are so interesting that collectors want to buy them, too.

Write T if the sentence is true, F if it is false, or NI if no information about the sentence is given in the video.

_____ a. Grenadians speak English.

_____ b. Many Grenadians write letters.

_____ c. Grenada produces its own stamps.

_____ d. The artists at the Philatela Company design many stamps with famous people on them.

_____ e. There are many stamp collectors in Grenada.

Crossword Puzzle

Across

1. The post office _____ letters and packages.
3. A _____ is strong, but it opens and closes easily.
7. _____ Hill, a British teacher, had the idea of putting glue on the back of postage stamps.
9. My pen is out of _____ .
10. The strips of cloth are flexible. They _____ easily.

Down

1. You have to _____ a feather pen in ink.
2. Every letter needs one of these.
4. Paid for in advance
5. There are five students in each _____ .
6. She still _____ me $10.
8. Same as #1 down

Dictionary Page

Finding Antonyms

Antonyms are words that have opposite meanings. For example, the words *hot* and *cold* are antonyms. When you look up a word in your dictionary, you can often find its antonym at the end of the definition.

> **accept** /ik'sept/ *verb*
> **1** to take willingly: *He accepted my apology for being late.*
> **2** to say yes to an invitation or offer: *Are you going to accept his invitation to the party?* (antonym) refuse

Write the antonym for each word. Use your dictionary to check your answers.

easy   _____

hate   _____

high   _____

receive   _____

slow   _____

wide   _____

together   _____

difficult   _____

Use one of the words from the list above in each of the following sentences.

1. These shoes are too big. They are the right length, but they are too _____.

2. The wall was so _____ that no one could get over it.

3. We are going to get the whole family _____ and have a big party.

4. She couldn't answer the question. It was much too _____.

5. This bus is very _____. We're going to be late to work.

Sports

Context Clues

Put a circle around the letter of the answer that means the same as the word or words in bold.

1. It is very cold in Norway in winter. You need a hat for your head and **gloves** for your hands.
   a. something to keep the hands warm
   b. something to make the hands look pretty
   c. something to cool the hands
   d. something that makes the hands work better

2. Captain Lee **trains** new police officers. The new officers study and practice for their new jobs.
   a. belongs to   c. agrees
   b. teaches   d. shaves

3. Oman is one of the Arab **nations.**
   a. countries   c. mountains
   b. religions   d. governors

4. Barbara had her coffee cup in front of her. When she finished drinking her coffee, she pushed the cup **aside.**
   a. off the table   c. into the kitchen
   b. to the side   d. into the air

5. Carol visited all the capital cities in Europe **except** Rome. She didn't have time to go there.
   a. when   c. but
   b. so   d. that

6. I'm sorry we can't talk any longer, but we are going to be late. We have to **rush.**
   a. move quickly   c. carry
   b. lead   d. grow

7. Switzerland has beautiful high mountains. However, people can't live high in the mountains because life there is too difficult. They live in the **valleys.**
   a. large cities on grasslands   c. low areas between mountains
   b. tropical forests   d. hot desert areas

8. I know there were **at least** fifty people there. Maybe there were more than that.
   - a. fewer than
   - b. no fewer than
   - c. about
   - d. more than

9. Only five people **participated in** the game. Everyone else was sick.
   - a. talked about
   - b. liked
   - c. played
   - d. bought

10. Pierre wrote an **excellent** composition. It is the best one in the class.
    - a. very, very good
    - b. not interesting
    - c. poor
    - d. boring

11. The teacher walked **ahead** of the students. He was leading the way to the new classroom.
    - a. in back of
    - b. near
    - c. beside
    - d. in front of

12. Coke and Pepsi are **similar** drinks. Seven-Up tastes different.
    - a. different
    - b. almost the same
    - c. opposite
    - d. identical

13. The Olympic Games **take place** every four years.
    - a. receive
    - b. happen
    - c. solve
    - d. decide

14. An **individual** can participate in the sport of running, but a team of people is needed to play soccer.
    - a. group of people
    - b. team
    - c. several people together
    - d. one person

Thai Boxing

© Luc Beziat/Stone/getty images

Before You Read

1. Are you familiar with the sport shown in the picture?

2. Can people use their knees in all kinds of boxing?

3. Do you think this sport is dangerous?

1 Thai Boxing

gloves

Boxing is popular in many countries. Two fighters wear boxing **gloves** on their hands. The boxers **hit** each other until one is knocked out or until the final bell rings. Each part of the fight is three minutes long. It is called a round.

Thai boxing is different.

The boxing **match** begins with music. Then the two fighters **kneel** and **pray** to God. Next, they do a slow dance that copies the movements of Thai boxing. During this dance, each fighter tries to show the other that he is best.

competition
bend down on the knees

Then the fight begins. In Thai boxing, the fighters can **kick** with their feet and hit each other with their **elbows** and knees. Of course, they hit with their hands, too. Each round is three minutes long. Then the boxers have a two-minute **rest.** Most boxers can fight only five rounds because this kind of fighting is very difficult.

hit with the feet
the part of the arm that bends

Thai boxing began over 500 years ago. If a soldier lost his **weapons** in a **battle,** he needed to fight with just his body. The soldiers learned how to use all the parts of their bodies. In 1560, the Burmese army **captured** Naresuen, the King of Thailand, in a war. King Naresuen was a very good boxer. He won his **freedom** from Burma by **defeating** all the best Burmese fighters. When he returned to Thailand, his people were very **proud** of him. Thai boxing became a popular sport.

fight

weapons

a Vocabulary

Put the right word in each blank. The sentences are from the text.

gloves	kneel	defeating	hit
match	weapons	elbows	pray
kick	captured	battle	
proud	rest	freedom	

1. The boxers _____ each other until one is knocked out.

2. The boxing _____ begins with music.

3. In Thai boxing, the fighters can _____ with their feet and hit each other with their _____ and knees.

4. Two fighters wear boxing _____ on their hands.

5. If a soldier lost his _____ in a _____, he needed to fight with just his body.

6. He won his _____ from Burma by _____ all the best Burmese fighters.

7. Then the two fighters _____ and _____ to God.

8. In 1560, the Burmese army _____ Naresuen, the King of Thailand, in a war.

9. When he returned to Thailand, his people were very _____ of him.

10. Then the boxers have a two-minute _____.

b Vocabulary: New Context

Put the right word in each blank.

match	freedom	captured	gloves
defeated	hit	pray	kick
kneel	battles	elbows	
weapons	rest	proud	

1. It is cold today. You should wear _____ and a hat.

2. Young children need a _____ in the afternoon.

3. There is a tennis _____ on television tomorrow afternoon.

4. You have to _____ down to pick up something that is on the floor.

44

5. The scientists _____ a dolphin so they could study it.

6. Your knees are part of your legs. Your _____ are part of your arms.

7. Religious people _____ every day.

8. Nadia got a good grade on her quiz. She is _____ of herself.

9. In soccer, you can _____ the ball. In basketball, you can't.

10. Most countries in the world spend too much money on _____ for their armies.

11. There are terrible _____ in a war.

12. Kenya was a British colony. It won its _____ in 1953.

13. The other team _____ us three times before we finally won a match.

14. The window broke when the ball _____ it.

C Vocabulary Review

Match each word in Column A with the word or phrase in Column B that means the same.

Column A	Column B
1. solve _____	a. line around the middle of the earth
2. object _____	b. anything
3. distance _____	c. the sister of a prince
4. revolution _____	d. the brother of a princess
5. equator _____	e. find an answer
6. whatever _____	f. war
7. princess _____	g. weather
8. independent _____	h. free
9. prince _____	i. how far one thing or place is from another
10. climate _____	j. thing

d Comprehension: Multiple Choice

Put a circle around the letter of the best answer.

1. A Thai boxing match begins with _____.
   - a. a prayer
   - c. music
   - b. a dance
   - d. a kick

2. Thai boxers don't hit with their _____.
   - a. hands
   - c. knees
   - b. elbows
   - d. heads

3. Thai boxers _____ before the fight.
   - a. grind
   - c. pray
   - b. knock out
   - d. capture

4. They pray on their _____.
   - a. elbows
   - c. hands
   - b. backs
   - d. knees

5. Thai boxing began_____.
   - a. as a sport
   - c. in the army
   - b. in the navy
   - d. as a dance

6. _____ made Thai boxing a popular sport.
   - a. A Burmese
   - c. A soldier
   - b. A king
   - d. The army

7. The king's people were _____.
   - a. proud of him
   - c. defeated
   - b. sad
   - d. captured

e Questions

The asterisk (*) means you have to think of the answer. You cannot find it in the text.

1. What do boxers wear on their hands?
2. What is one part of a fight called?
3. How does a Thai boxing match begin?
4. What do Thai boxers do before they start fighting?
*5. Why do they do a slow dance?
6. How is Thai boxing different from other kinds of boxing?
7. What is the length of a round in Thai boxing?
8. Why did Thai soldiers learn to box?

9. How did King Naresuen win his freedom?
10. How did his people feel about this?
*11. Is boxing safe or dangerous? Why?
*12. Is Thai boxing safer or more dangerous than other boxing? Why?

 **Main Idea**

Which is the main idea of this lesson? Choose one.

1. Thai boxing has music before the match.
2. Most Thai boxers can fight only a short time.
3. Thai boxing is different from other kinds of boxing.

Sumo Wrestling

© Hulton-Deutsch Collection/CORBIS

Before You Read

1. Are you familiar with the sport shown in the picture?

2. What is unusual about this sport?

3. What are the men trying to do to each other?

2   Sumo Wrestling

Sumo wrestling is a **national** sport in Japan. Every year there are six **tournaments,** and millions of Japanese watch them on television. A tournament is a <u>series</u> of matches.

one after another

Sumo is almost as old as the nation of Japan itself. Stories say that there was sumo wrestling over 2,000 years ago. There are written records of national sumo tournaments in the 8th century.

In many sports, <u>athletes</u> are thin and can move very quickly. However, sumo wrestlers weigh from 100 to 160 kilos (kilograms). One famous wrestler weighed 195 kilos. Sumo wrestlers do not move quickly, and sumo wrestling is a very slow sport.

people who play sports well

Sumo wrestlers start **training** when they are boys. They exercise to make their bodies **strong**. They also eat a lot.

They wrestle in a round **ring** with a sand floor. A wrestler loses the match if he leaves the ring. He is also the loser if any part of his body <u>except</u> his feet **touches** the floor. Each wrestler tries to push the other down on the floor or out of the ring. Sometimes one wrestler just **steps** <u>aside</u> when the other wrestler <u>rushes</u> toward him. Then, the wrestler who is rushing falls down or moves out of the ring.

but

aside = to the side
rushes = moves quickly

Sumo is not very popular in other countries, but the Japanese think that it is a very exciting sport.

a   Vocabulary

Put the right word in each blank. The sentences are from the text.

series	steps	touches	except
aside	national	training	tournaments
ring	athletes	rushes	strong

1. Sometimes one wrestler just _____ _____
   when the other wrestler _____ toward him.
2. A tournament is a _____ of matches.
3. He is also the loser if any part of his body _____ his feet
   _____ the floor.
4. Sumo wrestling is a _____ sport in Japan.
5. Sumo wrestlers start _____ when they are boys.
6. In many sports, _____ are thin and can move very quickly.
7. Every year there are six _____, and millions of Japanese
   watch them on television.
8. They wrestle in a round _____ with a sand floor.
9. They exercise to make their bodies _____.

b   Vocabulary: New Context

Put the right word in each blank.

athletes	stepped	series	national
ring	tournament	touch	train
rushed	except	aside	strong

1. Sumo wrestling is done in a round _____. Thai boxing is
   done in a square one.
2. You need _____ arms to lift something heavy.
3. Stan put his math homework _____. He said he would do
   it later.
4. _____ play basketball, lacrosse, volleyball, and many other
   kinds of sports.
5. Everyone _____ Amahl is in class today. She is absent.
6. What number is missing from this _____? 3, 6, 12, 15 . . .

7. The students are organizing a ping pong _____. Sign up if you want to play.

8. Marie _____ to class because she didn't want to be late.

9. In older elevators, you have to push a button to make the elevator go. In new ones, you just _____ the button.

10. Can you sing the _____ song of your country?

11. To be a good athlete, you need to _____ for a long time.

12. John _____ on a piece of paper that was on the floor.

c Vocabulary Review

Match the word in Column A with the word in Column B that means the opposite.

Column A		Column B
1. deliver	_____	a. later
2. capture	_____	b. stand up
3. accept	_____	c. empty
4. rest	_____	d. winner
5. together	_____	e. receive
6. loser	_____	f. apart
7. immediately	_____	g. refuse
8. embarrassed	_____	h. let go
9. kneel	_____	i. proud
10. fill	_____	j. work

d Comprehension: Multiple Choice

Put a circle around the letter of the best answer.

1. Every year there are _____ sumo tournaments in Japan.
   a. 6
   b. 15
   c. 160
   d. 195

2. There are written records of national sumo tournaments in the _____.
   a. Japanese sports center
   b. 1850s
   c. 8th century
   d. wrestling museum

3. Most athletes are _____.
   a. heavy   c. thin
   b. overweight   d. smooth

4. Sumo wrestlers are _____.
   a. small   c. thin
   b. heavy   d. smooth

5. Sumo wrestling is a _____ sport.
   a. fast   c. comfortable
   b. slow   d. efficient

6. Sumo wrestlers _____ to make their bodies strong.
   a. eat   c. lose
   b. swing   d. exercise

7. Each wrestler tries to push the other _____.
   a. down on the floor   c. into the air
   b. out of the ring   d. a or b

8. The Japanese think that sumo wrestling is _____.
   a. exciting   c. embarrassing
   b. boring   d. pleasant

 e Questions

The asterisk (*) means you have to think of the answer. You cannot find it in the text.

1. Where is sumo wrestling popular?
2. What is a tournament?
3. Is sumo wrestling an old sport?
4. How are sumo wrestlers different from other athletes?
5. How do sumo wrestlers train?
6. Describe a sumo ring.
7. How does a sumo wrestler lose a match?
*8. Is sumo wrestling exciting?
*9. Is it good for a person to weigh 160 or 195 kilos?

 f Main Idea

Which is the main idea of this lesson? Choose one.

1. Sumo wrestling is a popular traditional sport in Japan.
2. The sumo wrestling ring is round and has a sand floor.
3. A sumo match is slow, and the wrestlers are very large.

52

lesson

3

Tarahumara Foot Races

© Phil Schermeister/CORBIS

Before You Read

1. What do you know about the Tarahumara people from the picture?

2. One woman in the picture is carrying a stick. The other is carrying a ring. Can you guess why?

3. Do you like to run?

3   Tarahumara Foot Races

valley

The Tarahumara live in the mountains in the state of Chihuahua in northern Mexico. This is an area of high mountains and deep tropical **valleys.** It sometimes snows in the mountains in winter. There are not many roads.

The Tarahumara walk **wherever** they need to go.   anywhere
They carry heavy baskets on their **backs.** Perhaps this is why the Tarahumara can **run** many kilometers without getting tired. They are **excellent** runners, and they like   very good
to organize races.

When the men race, they kick a wooden ball **ahead**   in front
of them while they run. Before they start racing, they **plan** where and how long they will run. They might run just a few minutes, or they might run for several hours. Sometimes they run in teams, and sometimes each person runs as an **individual.**   one person

The women's races are **similar** except that the   almost the same
women do not kick a ball. They **throw** a wooden hoop in front of them with a stick. A hoop is a ring, or a **circle.**

The Tarahumara play other games and sports. However, they are famous because they can run so fast and so far.

a   Vocabulary

Put the right word in each blank. The sentences are from the text.

excellent	ahead	wherever	throw
run	circle	plan	valleys
backs	similar	individual	

1. Perhaps this is why the Tarahumara can _____ many kilometers without getting tired.
2. When the men race, they kick a wooden ball _____ of them while they run.
3. This is an area of high mountains and deep tropical _____.
4. They are _____ runners, and they like to organize races.
5. They carry heavy baskets on their _____.
6. The women's races are _____ except that the women do not kick a ball.
7. They _____ a wooden hoop in front of them with a stick.
8. Sometimes they run in teams, and sometimes each person runs as an _____.
9. The Tarahumara walk _____ they need to go.
10. Before they start racing, they _____ where and how long they will run.
11. A hoop is a ring, or a _____.

Lesson 3: Tarahumara Foot Races

b Vocabulary: New Context

Put the right word in each blank.

circle	individually	run	wherever
valley	backs	excellent	threw
similar	ahead	planned	

1. The teacher told the children to hold hands and form a large _____.

2. A sumo wrestler and a runner are both athletes, but they are not _____ in size.

3. Horses can carry a lot on their _____.

4. As Betty and Pat drove along the highway, they could see beautiful mountains _____ of them.

5. A _____ is a low area between two mountains.

6. Sometimes students answer questions in a group, and sometimes they answer _____.

7. Masako is an _____ student. She always gets good grades.

8. You will find English speakers _____ you go.

9. She _____ some important papers in the trash by mistake.

10. I _____ to get up early yesterday morning, but I didn't get up until 10.

11. How far can you _____?

c Vocabulary Review

Put the right word in each blank.

weapon	athletes	except	aside
series	elbows	freedom	held
proud	touch	strong	shape

1. When the children came in the room, their father put his book _____.

2. In some countries, the people do not have the _____ to speak against the government.

3. She _____ the child's hand as they walked across the bridge.

4. A basketball is not the same _____ as an American football.

5. There are _____ from several countries in the competition for the World Cup.

6. Can you _____ your toes with your hands?

7. A stick or a stone can be a _____.

8. Is it polite to put your _____ on the table?

9. Do all of the exercises _____ the last one. Don't do that one.

10. The first unit in this book has a _____ of lessons on inventions.

11. A runner needs to have _____ legs.

12. He is very _____ of his daughter. She works very hard and helps the family a lot.

d Comprehension: True/False/No Information

Write T *if the sentence is true. Write* F *if it is false. Write* NI *if no information about the sentence was given in the text.*

_____ 1. Chihuahua is a state in Mexico.

_____ 2. It is hot in the valleys where the Tarahumara live.

_____ 3. They get a lot of exercise.

_____ 4. They often travel by car.

_____ 5. They cook their food outdoors.

_____ 6. The Tarahumara men are excellent runners, but the women are not.

_____ 7. The winners of the races receive money.

_____ 8. They usually race down the mountains.

_____ 9. The women kick a ball as they race.

_____ 10. The Tarahumara are famous because they are good wrestlers.

 57

Questions

The asterisk (*) means you have to think of the answer. You cannot find it in the text.

1. Where do the Tarahumara live?
2. What is the land like there?
3. Does it ever snow?
4. How do they travel?
5. Describe how the men race.
6. Do they always run in teams?
7. How is a women's race different from a men's race?
8. What is a hoop?
*9. Why are the Tarahumara excellent runners?

 Main Idea

Which is the main idea of this lesson? Choose one.

1. The Tarahumara live in the state of Chihuahua in Mexico.
2. The Tarahumara are excellent runners.
3. The Tarahumara women's races are similar to the men's.

Olympic Sports

Before You Read

1. Do you like to watch the Olympic Games on television? What are your favorite sports in the Olympics?

2. What sports are not in the Olympic Games? Do you think that they should be?

3. Do you think we should continue to have the Olympics? Why or why not?

4   Olympic Sports

The first modern Olympic Games **took place** in Athens, Greece, in the year 1896. Athletes from only 13 countries **participated** in the Games that year. They competed in 43 different **events** in just 9 sports (track and field, swimming, cycling, fencing, gymnastics, shooting, tennis, weight lifting, and wrestling). In 2004, the summer Olympic Games took place once again in Athens, Greece. This time athletes from 202 countries competed in 300 events in 28 sports.

Only five sports have been in every Olympic Games. They are track and field, swimming, fencing, cycling, and gymnastics. Other sports come and go in the Olympic Games. For example, tennis was an Olympic sport from 1896 until 1924. Then it disappeared from the Olympics until 1988. Baseball, badminton, and taekwondo are more **recent** additions to the Olympic Games.

It is the job of the International Olympic **Committee** (IOC) to add and <u>remove</u> sports from the Olympic Games. A sport has to be popular in <u>at least</u> 50 countries on three continents before it can be added. However, the IOC doesn't want to add more sports to the Olympic Games without <u>eliminating</u> others. The IOC is afraid that there will be too many sports in the Olympics.

Artistic events were also a part of the Olympic Games from 1912 to 1948. There were **contests** in architecture, music, literature, and painting. Today some people think that artistic events and games such as chess should be part of the Olympics. However, many people <u>oppose</u> this idea.

The Olympic Games today are very different from the first modern Olympic Games in 1896. These differences **reflect** the changing definition and popularity of sports.

take out

no fewer than

taking out, removing

be against

60

a | Vocabulary

Put the right word in each blank. The sentences are from the text.

eliminating	remove	recent	committee
participated	at least	took place	oppose
contests	events	reflect	

1. Baseball, badminton, and taekwondo are more _____ additions to the Olympic Games.

2. Athletes from only 13 countries _____ in the Games that year.

3. It is the job of the International Olympic _____ (IOC) to add and _____ sports from the Olympic Games.

4. The first modern Olympic Games _____ in Athens, Greece, in the year 1896.

5. However, the IOC doesn't want to add more sports to the Olympic Games without _____ others.

6. These differences _____ the changing definition and popularity of sports.

7. The first Olympic athletes competed in 43 different _____ in just 9 sports.

8. A sport has to be popular in _____ 50 countries on three continents before it can be added.

9. There were _____ in architecture, music, literature, and painting.

10. However, many people _____ this idea.

61

b Vocabulary: New Context

Put the right word in each blank.

at least	eliminate	participate	removed
committee	event	recently	take place
contest	opposed	reflection	

1. When does your favorite holiday _____?

2. I went to the beach last month, but I haven't gone anywhere
   _____.

3. What problems do we need to _____ from the world?

4. Do you know why they _____ my name from the door?

5. How many people are there on the _____?

6. We have a speech _____ in our class every year.

7. Did you study _____ thirty minutes yesterday?

8. Do you _____ in any sports right now?

9. Ten students wanted to have a class trip, but eight students
   _____ the idea. They didn't want to take a trip.

10. Their wedding was a big _____ for everyone in the family.

11. I can see your _____ in the window.

c Vocabulary Review

Underline the word that does not belong in each group.

1. walk, throw, kick, run
2. engineer, carpenter, inventor, prince
3. take place, mail, send, deliver
4. runner, wrestler, boxer, member
5. elbow, knee, oppose, leg
6. climate, tournament, match, contest
7. hit, kick, touch, rush
8. rest, train, compete, participate

d Comprehension: Multiple Choice

Put a circle around the letter of the best answer.

1. The first modern Olympic Games took place _____.
   a. before 1896   b. in 1896   c. recently   d. 50 years ago

2. There are _____ sports in the Olympics today than in the past.
   a. the same number of   b. more   c. fewer   d. more difficult

3. Baseball _____ an Olympic sport.
   a. was never   b. is not now   c. was always   d. is now

4. _____ want to add games such as chess to the Olympics.
   a. IOC members   b. Most athletes   c. Some people   d. Artists

5. A sport that was eliminated from the Olympics and later included again is _____.
   a. tennis   b. taekwondo   c. chess   d. music

6. In the past, the Olympics included contests in _____.
   a. painting   b. architecture   c. music   d. a, b, and c

7. It is the job of the International Olympic Committee to _____ sports.
   a. play   b. plan   c. eliminate   d. watch

8. More athletes _____ the Olympics now than in the past.
   a. participate in   b. oppose   c. train for   d. a and c

e Questions

The asterisk (*) means you have to think of the answer. You cannot find it in the text.

1. How were the 1896 Olympic Games different from the 2004 Games?
*2. Why did only 13 nations participate in the 1896 Games?
*3. Why did the Olympic Committee eliminate tennis after 1924?
4. What is the IOC?
5. What kinds of artistic events were in the Olympics?
*6. Why did artistic events disappear from the Games?
*7. What is a game besides chess that might be included in future Olympics?

f Main Idea

What is the main idea of this lesson? Choose one.

1. Only five sports have been in every Olympic Games.
2. The Olympics today are very different from the first Olympics.
3. Different sports are popular today than in the past.

Great Athletes

© Bettmann/CORBIS

Before You Read

1. What sport is the athlete in the picture participating in?

2. What qualities do you need to be successful in this sport?

3. Did you ever run in a race?

5   Great Athletes

You might think that Olympic athletes are the healthiest people in the world. It's true that many are. However, it's also true that **quite a few** Olympic athletes had to **overcome** illnesses early in their lives.

many

One excellent example is Wilma Rudolph. She competed in track-and-field events in the 1960 Olympics. She didn't win just one gold **medal.** She won three. At the time, people called her "the fastest woman in the world."

↳ medal

As a young child, Wilma Rudolph could not participate in sports. She had a series of **serious** illnesses, and then, at the age of 4, she got polio. She lost the use of her left leg, and the doctors said she would never walk again.

important

The people in Rudolph's family did everything they could to help her walk again. Wilma and her mother **frequently** traveled 100 miles to get **treatments** for her leg. Her brothers and sisters **took turns** giving her leg a daily massage. Four times a day, they helped her do special exercises for her leg. **Amazingly,** by the time Rudolph was 9 years old, she was able to walk again. Before long, she started playing basketball and running. In high school, she was a track star, and then she went to the Olympics.

often
medical help

Wilma Rudolph **retired** from her **career** as a runner when she was 22 years old. She then became a teacher and track **coach.** Her story **encouraged** many people to work hard and to overcome difficulties.

profession

trainer

 65

a Vocabulary

Put the right word in each blank. The sentences are from the text.

amazingly	career	overcome	retired
medal	frequently	treatments	took turns
quite a few	encouraged	coach	serious

1. However, it's also true that _____ Olympic athletes had to _____ illnesses early in their lives.

2. She had a series of _____ illnesses, and then, at the age of 4, she got polio.

3. _____, by the time Rudolph was 9 years old, she was able to walk again.

4. Her story _____ many people to work hard and to overcome difficulties.

5. Wilma and her mother _____ traveled 100 miles to get _____ for her leg.

6. Wilma Rudolph _____ from her _____ as a runner when she was 22 years old.

7. Her brothers and sisters _____ giving her leg a daily massage.

8. She then became a teacher and track _____.

9. She didn't win just one gold _____.

b Vocabulary: New Context

Put the right word in each blank.

amazing	encouraged	overcome	serious
career	frequently	quite a few	take turns
coach	medal	retire	treatments

1. _____ people _____ at age 65.

2. My trainer _____ me to compete in the tournament.

3. Engineering is a good _____.

4. Let's _____ telling a story. You go first.

5. I heard an _____ story. It's difficult to believe.

6. My teacher is sick, but it isn't anything _____. She'll be back at work soon.

7. In many sports events, the winner gets a special cup or a _____.

8. My trainer _____ participates in sports events.

9. What is the most difficult thing you had to _____ in your childhood?

10. Every year scientists find new _____ for serious illnesses.

11. A good _____ can help you become a better athlete.

C Vocabulary Review

Match the word in Column A with the word in Column B that means the same.

Column A		**Column B**
1. trainer	_____	a. very good
2. remove	_____	b. ring
3. reflect	_____	c. defeat
4. excellent	_____	d. in front
5. retire	_____	e. eliminate
6. take place	_____	f. coach
7. ahead	_____	g. strong
8. circle	_____	h. show
9. athletic	_____	i. stop working
10. win	_____	j. happen

d Comprehension: Multiple Choice

Put a circle around the letter of the best answer.

1. Wilma Rudolph was _____ when she was a child.
   a. healthy   c. sick
   b. strong   d. retired

2. When she was a child, she couldn't use her _____.
   a. leg   c. hand
   b. elbow   d. arm

3. She won _____ in the 1960 Olympics.
   a. a gold medal   c. quite a few medals
   b. a silver medal   d. three gold medals

4. Polio was a _____ illness.
   a. proud   c. serious
   b. recent   d. strong

5. The people in Wilma Rudolph's family were very _____.
   a. retired   c. serious
   b. helpful   d. fast

6. _____ one of her brothers or sisters massaged her leg.
   a. Sometimes   c. Every day
   b. Once a week   d. Once in awhile

7. Rudolph had a _____ career as a runner.
   a. long   c. restful
   b. short   d. lengthy

8. Rudolph had to travel _____ to get treatments for her leg.
   a. alone   c. a long distance
   b. frequently d. b and c

e Questions

The asterisk (*) means you have to think of the answer. You cannot find it in the text.

*1. How would you describe Wilma Rudolph?
 2. What was difficult about her life?
*3. How did she overcome polio?
 4. How did her family help with her treatments?
 5. What sports did she participate in?
*6. Why do you think she retired from her career as a runner at age 22?
*7. Do you know anyone similar to her?

f Main Idea

Which is the main idea of this lesson? Choose one.

1. Wilma Rudolph was a great Olympic athlete, coach, and teacher.
2. Wilma Rudolph overcame many difficulties to become a great athlete.
3. Wilma Rudolph's family helped her overcome polio.

a Map Study

These are the seven continents: Africa, Antarctica, Asia, Australia, Europe, North America, and South America. Tell which continent each place is located on.

a. Sweden   _____

b. Thailand   _____

c. France   _____

d. China   _____

e. Argentina   _____

f. India   _____

g. Miramar (Burma)   _____

h. Great Britain   _____

i. Canada   _____

j. the South Pole   _____

b Compound Words

Use a word from Column A and a word from Column B to make a compound word. Sometimes you can make two words that begin with a word in Column A. The first one is done for you.

Column A		Column B
1. birth	*birthday*	a. mate
2. table	_____	b. event
3. day	_____	c. member
4. bed	_____	d. cloth
5. summer	_____	e. light
6. room	_____	f. day
7. class	_____	g. rise
8. team	_____	h. time
9. sun	_____	i. room

C Word Forms

Verb	Noun	Adjective
1. cube	cube	cubic
2. move	movement	movable
3. (none)	athlete	athletic
4. free	freedom	free
5. amaze	amazement	amazing
6. (none)	nation, nationality	national
7. rest	rest	restful
8. think	thought	thoughtful
9. run	running, runner	running
10. strengthen	strength	strong

Put the correct word form in each blank. Use words from line 1 in item 1, and so on. Use the right verb forms and singular or plural nouns.

1. What is a _____? What does a _____ gram of water weigh?

2. A zipper _____ up and down. Each _____ opens or closes the zipper.

3. I'm not a very _____ person. Are you an _____?

4. The Burmese captured King Naresuen. He won his _____ by boxing. When he was _____, he returned to Thailand.

5. Who is the most _____ person you know? What about this person _____ you?

6. Where are you from? What is your _____? What does your _____ flag look like?

7. When you want to _____, we can go inside. It's very _____ there.

8. What are you _____ about? Is your family in your _____ often?

9. Tom _____ 5 kilometers every morning. He is a fast _____. _____ is good for him.

10. He has _____ arms, but he doesn't have

much _____ in his legs. He needs to

_____ his legs.

d Past Tense Review

Write the past tense of each verb.

1. step _____   6. try _____
2. receive _____   7. capture _____
3. mail _____   8. touch _____
4. seem _____   9. defeat _____
5. plan _____   10. oppose _____

e Irregular Verbs

Memorize these verbs. Then use the past tense in a sentence.

Simple	Past
1. throw	threw
2. pay	paid
3. slide	slid
4. hit	hit
5. overcome	overcame
6. run	ran
7. take place	took place
8. bend	bent
9. hold	held

f Writing

Choose one or more of these topics and write answers.

1. Which sport in Unit 2 is most interesting to you? Why?
2. Do you have a favorite sport? Do you play it or only watch it? What do you like about it?
3. In the United States, famous athletes in some popular sports—for example, football and baseball—earn a lot of money. In your country, do any famous athletes earn a lot of money? Who pays them? Do you think it is a good idea for famous athletes to earn a lot of money? Why or why not?

Video Highlights

a Before You Watch

Look at the picture. Answer the questions.

1. Have you ever played this game?
2. Do you think this game is a sport? Why or why not?
3. Is this a game you "play for fun" or "play to win"?

b As You Watch

1. *Scrabble® is a vocabulary game. You have seven letters and you make words on a board. Circle the things you think Scrabble® players do during a game. Watch the video and check.*

touch	pick up	hold	jump
rest	solve	kick	write

2. *Write the correct number in each sentence.*

   97   25,000   12   50   850   93   5 or 6

   a. There are _____ Scrabble® experts at the competition from _____ different countries.

   b. The age range is from _____ years old to _____ years old.

   c. There are _____ legal two-letter words in Scrabble®.

   d. You get _____ points for putting down a seven-letter word.

   e. The top prize is $_____.

C After You Watch

1. *What skills do you need to be good at Scrabble®, sumo, and soccer? Check the boxes.*

You need . . .	Scrabble®	Sumo	Soccer
a. lots of luck	☐	☐	☐
b. lots of training	☐	☐	☐
c. to be very strong	☐	☐	☐
d. good concentration	☐	☐	☐
e. good memory	☐	☐	☐
f. excellent word skills	☐	☐	☐

2. *Use the Scrabble® letters below to make new words. For example, you could take the letter "I" and the letter "S" to make the word "IS."*

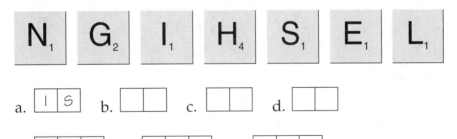

a. $\boxed{I\ S}$ b. ☐☐ c. ☐☐ d. ☐☐

e. ☐☐☐ f. ☐☐☐ g. ☐☐☐

h. ☐☐☐☐☐☐☐ (*Hint*: What you are studying now!)

3. *How many points do your words make?*

Example: IS (I = 1, S = 1) = 1 + 1 = 2 points.

Activity Page

a Sporting Needs

What do you need to play each of these sports?

tennis   basketball   baseball   soccer

For each sport, choose two or more items from those shown below. Some items will be used more than once. Then write a sentence for each sport.

Example: To play tennis, you need a ball, a racket, and a court.

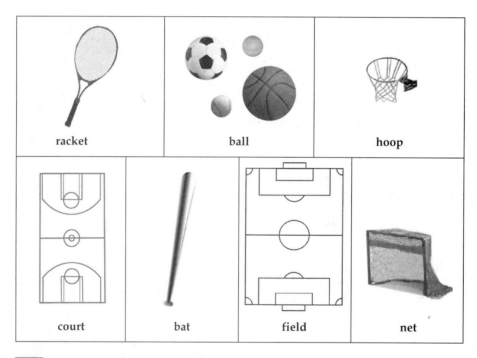

racket	ball	hoop
court	bat	field	net

b What Sport Do I Play?

Read one of your sentences from part a above to a partner, without identifying the sport. Your partner tries to guess the sport.

Example: To play this sport, you need a court, a net, and a ball.

You can also do this activity with sports that are not listed above.

Stress and Pronunciation

1. **Stress.** If a word has more than one syllable, one of the syllables is stronger than the others. Your dictionary always has a stress mark (') in front of the stressed syllable. In the words below, say whether the stress is on the first, second, or third syllable. The first one is done for you.

'popular ___1___	'probably _____	ex'cept _____
'exercise _____	scien'tific _____	de'feated _____
'national _____	a'nother _____	'organize _____
a'side _____	un'usual _____	refu'gee _____

2. **Pronunciation.** The strange writing you see on this page is *phonetics*. Your dictionary includes a guide to pronunciation symbols, which shows how to read phonetics. The phonetic spelling of a word is between the two slanted lines / / following each main entry. Look at the two entries below and write their normal spelling in the space provided.

_____
/'fridəm/ *noun*
1 having the power to act and speak without being stopped: *The boy has the freedom to go where he wants to go.*

_____
/raʊnd/ *adjective*
circular or curved in shape: *Balls are round.*

Now match the words in phonetics with the words in normal spelling.
The first one is done for you.

Phonetic Spelling

1. /glʌvz/ _____f. gloves_____
2. /ˈsaidwɔk/ _____
3. /streit/ _____
4. /ˈɛlboʊ/ _____
5. /flæt/ _____
6. /ˈkæptən/ _____
7. /drʌm/ _____
8. /ˈfridəm/ _____
9. /raʊnd/ _____
10. /mætʃ/ _____

Normal Spelling

a. round
b. match
c. drum
d. sidewalk
e. straight
f. gloves
g. freedom
h. elbow
i. captain
j. flat

Each sentence contains one word in phonetics. The word is given in its
normal spelling as one of the three words that follow the sentence.
Choose the correct word and underline it.

1. The men /kɪk/ a wooden ball. (hit, kick, stick)
2. Athletes from /θərˈtin/ countries participated in the Games.
   (thirteen, thirty, three)
3. No part of his body except his feet touches the /flɔr/.
   (flat, floor, flute)
4. Young people find this traditional /spɔrt/ exciting.
   (sport, spirit, speed)
5. Sumo /ˈresliŋ/ is a Japanese sport.
   (rushing, rusting, wrestling)

Food

Context Clues

Put a circle around the letter of the answer that means the same as the word or words in bold.

1. Betty hated her glasses, so she broke them **on purpose.**
   a. not by accident
   b. on the floor
   c. on the next day
   d. without thinking

2. Your face is **familiar** to me, but I don't remember your name.
   a. unknown
   b. unusual
   c. known
   d. far away

3. There are only a few **ingredients** in the bread: flour, water, yeast, and a little sugar.
   a. mixtures
   b. spices
   c. things that are mixed to cook something
   d. values

4. You can look in today's newspaper to **find out** the weather for tomorrow.
   a. deliver
   b. plan
   c. eliminate
   d. learn

5. That wooden desk is **solid** oak. It will last for hundreds of years.
   a. thin
   b. mostly
   c. not real
   d. all

6. Our bus broke down on the highway, but **eventually** another bus came to get us. When we finally got home, we were only 4 hours late.
   a. immediately
   b. after a short time
   c. sometime later
   d. frequently

7. That painting of her children didn't cost much money, but she **values** it more than anything else in the house.
   a. uses
   b. cares about it
   c. hates
   d. wants to sell it

78

8. The last dodo bird died many years ago. Now this kind of bird is **extinct.**
   a. eliminated   c. far away
   b. serious   d. strong

9. When there is a **shortage** of food, people often start fighting among themselves.
   a. extra   c. not enough
   b. cheap   d. good

10. I tried to catch the ball, but I **missed** it, and it went over the fence.
    a. found   c. didn't get
    b. got   d. touched

11. We usually have sunny weather at this time of year. It's **rare** to have rain.
    a. common   c. serious
    b. expected   d. uncommon

12. He **took a risk** when he ran into the burning house. He's lucky he didn't die.
    a. did something funny   c. did something easy
    b. did something dangerous d. did something common

Context Clues

The Puffer Fish

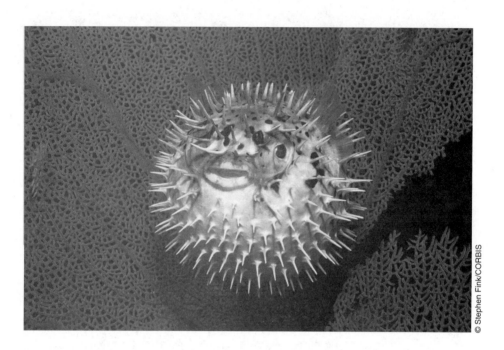

© Stephen Fink/CORBIS

Before You Read

1. The fish in the picture has spines all over its body. What might be the purpose of the spines?

2. Why do you think it's called the puffer fish?

3. Do you have a favorite fish dish? What is it?

1   The Puffer Fish

Most people **<u>avoid</u>** eating dangerous foods. They don't want to get sick. However, there is one food that can be deadly, **yet** some people eat it **on purpose.** It's called the puffer fish.

stay away from

This kind of fish, called *fugu* in Japanese, lives in the Pacific Ocean. Some people die every year from eating *fugu*. In fact, the Emperor of Japan is not allowed to touch it. Why? Well, the insides of the puffer fish are very poisonous. They **contain** a poison 275 times more **<u>powerful</u>** than the deadly poison cyanide.

strong

Usually nothing bad happens when *fugu* is on a restaurant's menu. **Customers** feel great after the meal. That's because chefs are trained to remove the insides of the puffer fish before they give it to customers. If they **miss** even a small **amount,** the fish is not safe to eat.

Puffer fish is very expensive. A plate of *fugu* costs more than $200 in some restaurants in Tokyo. **<u>Besides</u>** being dangerous to eat, the fish is very ugly, with spines all over its body. Also, it can puff, or blow, itself up to **double** its **<u>normal</u>** size. Why do the Japanese **risk** so much for such an ugly and dangerous fish? Well, some people like taking risks. And *fugu* tastes wonderful.

also, in addition to

usual

a Vocabulary

Put the right word in each blank. The sentences are from the text.

avoid	contain	customers	on purpose	miss	normal
besides	risk	amount	double	yet	powerful

1. _____ feel great after the meal.
2. However, there is one food that can be deadly, _____ some people eat it _____.
3. Why do the Japanese _____ so much for such an ugly and dangerous fish?
4. They _____ a poison 275 times more _____ than the deadly poison cyanide.
5. Most people _____ eating dangerous foods.
6. Also, it can puff, or blow, itself up to _____ its _____ size.
7. If they _____ even a small _____, the fish is not safe to eat.
8. _____ being dangerous to eat, the fish is very ugly, with spines all over its body.

b Vocabulary: New Context

Put the right word in each blank.

besides	avoids	amount	on purpose	yet	powerful
contained	risks	customers	missed	double	normal

1. Heavy snow is _____ for Iceland at this time of year.
2. Peanuts make him sick, so he _____ eating them.
3. Henry said he hit me by accident, but I know he did it _____.
4. I _____ three balls during the soccer game, but we still won.
5. She received a package from her family that _____ food and clothes.
6. He took so many bad _____ with money that he was penniless in a year.

82

7. She may look shy and weak, but they say she's one of the most
   _____ people in banking.

8. Five people live in my house _____ me.

9. The two couples went to the movies together on a _____ date.

10. The _____ of money you save depends on how much you earn.

11. He said he wasn't hungry, _____ he ate a whole pizza by himself.

12. So many _____ ate at Luigi's restaurant on the first evening that he decided to get a second chef.

C Vocabulary Review

Put the right word in each blank.

similar	gloves	touch	individual
trained	excellent	tournament	metric
grind	recent	distance	take turns

1. To make coffee, you need to _____ the beans first.

2. What is the _____ from the earth to the moon?

3. My parents _____ helping the children with their homework.

4. Did you hear the most _____ news from Mexico?

5. Can I borrow your _____? Mine are lost and my hands are freezing.

6. The dresses are _____. They are the same color and style, but Nancy's has a belt.

7. There was a tennis _____ that day, but Philip had a cold and couldn't play.

8. Her written work was _____, but she failed the oral test.

9. She _____ as a ballet dancer for five years before she appeared on stage.

10. "Please don't _____ the cake," their mother warned. "It's for our guests."

11. I want to learn the _____ system of measurement before I go to France next year.

12. One _____ walked out of the movie theater after an hour.

Comprehension: True/False/No Information

Write T *if the sentence is true. Write* F *if it is false. Write* NI *if no information about the sentence was given in the text.*

_____ 1. Puffer fish is popular in Japan.
_____ 2. The Emperor of Japan eats *fugu* for his evening meal.
_____ 3. The most dangerous part of the puffer fish is its spines.
_____ 4. The puffer fish lives in the Pacific Ocean.
_____ 5. *Fugu* is popular because it is very cheap.
_____ 6. This fish can puff itself up to ten times its normal size.
_____ 7. There is some risk in eating a plate of *fugu*.
_____ 8. It is called the puffer fish in English because of the spines that cover its body.
_____ 9. The insides of the puffer fish are very poisonous.
_____ 10. A few restaurants in New York serve *fugu*.

 Questions

The asterisk (*) means you have to think of the answer. You cannot find it in the text.

1. In what ocean does the puffer fish live?
*2. Is this ocean near Japan?
3. What parts of the puffer fish are poisonous?
4. Can the Emperor of Japan eat puffer fish? Why or why not?
5. What is cyanide?
6. In which country is *fugu* most popular?
7. What must chefs do before they serve puffer fish?
8. How much does a plate of *fugu* cost in some restaurants?
*9. Why do you think *fugu* costs so much?
*10. Why do you think the puffer fish has spines all over its body?

f Main Idea

Which is the main idea of this lesson? Choose one.

1. *Fugu* is one of the most expensive foods in the world.
2. Some people are willing to risk their lives to eat *fugu*.
3. Chefs must be carefully trained to prepare puffer fish for customers.

lesson 2

Foods from Around the World

Before You Read

1. Which of the following would you use to eat the food in each picture: chopsticks, fingers, or knives and forks?

2. Which meal looks the most enjoyable? Why?

3. People spend a lot of time talking about food. Why do you think this is so?

2 Foods from Around the World

Foods that are well known to you may not be **familiar** to people from other countries. Tourists and other travelers almost always get to try some unfamiliar food. That is part of the fun of traveling. Here are four people's **experiences** with **foreign** food.

common, well-known

Shao Wong is a student in France. He comes from China. "I never had cheese or even milk before I came to France. Cattle are **rare** in my part of China, so there are no **dairy** products. I drank some milk when I first arrived in France. I hated it! I tried cheese, too, but I didn't like it. I love ice cream, though, and that's made from milk."

uncommon

containing milk or related to cows

Birgit is from Sweden. She traveled to Australia on vacation. "I was in a restaurant that specialized in fish, and I heard some other customers **order** flake. So I ordered some, too, and it was **delicious**. Later, I **found out** that flake is an Australian **term** for shark. Now, whenever I see a new food, I try it on purpose. You know why? I remember how much I enjoyed flake."

tastes good

learned

Chandra is a dentist in Texas. She is from India. "I'm afraid to try new foods because they might contain beef. I'm a Hindu, and my religion **forbids** me to eat meat from the cow. That's why I can't eat hamburgers or spaghetti with meatballs."

Nathan is from the United States. He taught for a year in China. "My friends gave me some 100-year-old eggs to eat. I didn't like their appearance at all. The eggs were green inside, but my friends said the color was normal. The Chinese put **chemicals** on fresh eggs. Then they **bury** them in the earth for three months. So the eggs weren't really very old. Even so, I didn't want to touch them."

Life in a new country can be **scary,** but it also can be fun. Would you eat a 100-year-old egg? Would you order shark in a restaurant?

frightening

86

a Vocabulary

Put the right word in each blank. The sentences are from the text.

chemicals	delicious	order	found out
forbids	rare	dairy	bury
experiences	term	familiar	foreign
scary			

1. Cattle are _____ in my part of China, so there are no _____ products.

2. So I ordered some, too, and it was _____.

3. Then they _____ them in the earth for three months.

4. Foods that are well known to you may not be _____ to people from other countries.

5. Life in a new country can be _____, but it also can be fun.

6. I'm a Hindu, and my religion _____ me to eat meat from the cow.

7. I was in a restaurant that specialized in fish, and I heard some other customers _____ flake.

8. Here are four people's _____ with _____ food.

9. The Chinese put _____ on fresh eggs.

10. Later, I _____ that flake is an Australian _____ for shark.

b Vocabulary: New Context

Put the right word in each blank.

familiar	scared	term	find out
forbids	delicious	dairy	rarely
experience	chemicals	buried	order
foreign			

1. My school _____ gum chewing in class.

2. The loud noise _____ everyone in the room.

3. Many people don't know that a lot of household cleaners contain dangerous _____.

4. How did you _____ what my telephone number is? I didn't give it to anyone.

5. My brother coached the soccer team for several years. He also has _____ coaching basketball and baseball.

6. Ice cream is a _____ product, and so is cheese.

7. When our cat died, we _____ him under the apple tree.

8. If we _____ a computer from that store, we'll get a month's supply of computer paper free.

9. Zampa's is a popular restaurant because the food is always _____.

10. We don't use the _____ *housewife* any more. Many women don't like it.

11. I often take the train to work, but I _____ take the bus.

12. "His face looks _____ to me," said Arthur. "I've probably met him somewhere before."

13. Can you speak any _____ languages?

c Vocabulary Review

Match the word in Column A with the word in Column B that means the same. The first one is done for you.

Column A

1. series — *g. a group of similar events*
2. contest _____
3. remove _____
4. frequently _____
5. customer _____
6. normal _____
7. career _____
8. rush _____
9. risk _____
10. except _____
11. avoid _____
12. powerful _____

Column B

a. take away
b. move quickly
c. buyer
d. stay away from
e. danger
f. all but
g. a group of similar events
h. strong
i. profession
j. average
k. competition
l. often

d Comprehension: Multiple Choice

Put a circle around the letter of the best answer.

1. Some foods of other countries might be _____ to you.
   a. unfamiliar
   b. recent
   c. similar
   d. proud

2. The Hindu religion forbids the eating of _____.
   a. green vegetables
   b. chemicals
   c. beef
   d. candy

3. Shao Wong wasn't familiar with _____ before he went to France.
   a. meat
   b. beef
   c. dairy products
   d. flake

4. Hundred-year-old eggs are really only _____ old.
   a. three months   c. three years
   b. thirty days   d. three decades

5. In Australia, *flake* is another word for _____.
   a. octopus   c. cheese
   b. hamburger   d. shark

6. Ice cream is made from _____.
   a. cheese   c. milk
   b. cattle   d. fish

7. The insides of 100-year-old eggs are _____.
   a. green   c. yellow
   b. white   d. grey

8. Chandra can't eat beef because of her _____.
   a. family   c. religion
   b. health   d. salary

 e Questions

The asterisk (*) means you have to think of the answer. You cannot find it in the text.

 1. Where does Shao Wong come from?
 2. What foods did he sample when he first arrived in France?
 3. Why did Birgit go to Australia?
*4. Do people from Sweden eat shark?
 5. Why does Birgit like to try new foods?
 6. Why is Chandra afraid to try new foods?
 7. Do Hindus eat beef? Why or why not?
 8. Where is Nathan from?
 9. Why didn't he want to touch 100-year-old eggs?
10. How do the Chinese make 100-year-old eggs?
11. What was the real age of the Chinese eggs?
*12. Do people in China eat a lot of butter?

f Main Idea

Which is the main idea of this lesson? Choose one.

1. People from different countries do things differently.
2. Foods that are familiar to you might be unfamiliar to foreigners.
3. Many people dislike eating new foods because their religion forbids it.

lesson

3

Chocolate

Before You Read

1. The two pictures are connected in some way. How?

2. Can you name some foods that use chocolate?

3. When did you last eat something with chocolate in it? What was it?

3   Chocolate

We think of chocolate as something sweet. However, a long time ago, people thought of chocolate as something very **bitter.** For us, chocolate is a candy, but **once** it was a medicine. Today, chocolate can be a hot drink, a frozen **dessert,** or just a **snack.** Sometimes it's an **ingredient** in the main course of a meal. Mexicans make a hot chocolate sauce called *mole* and **pour** it over chicken. The Mexicans also eat chocolate with spices like chili peppers.

Chocolate is a product of the tropical cacao tree. Cacao beans taste so bitter that even monkeys say "ugh!" and run away. The word *chocolate* comes from a Mayan word. The Mayas were an **ancient** people who once lived in Mexico. They **valued** the cacao tree. Some of the Mayas used cacao beans for money, while others ground them to make a bitter drink.

When the Spaniards came to Mexico in the 16th century, they started drinking cacao, too. Because the drink was strong and bitter, they thought it was a medicine. When the Spaniards took the drink back to Europe, people **discovered** that sugar removed the bitter taste of cacao. **Wealthy** Spaniards heated the sweet drink and thought that it was good for their health.

In the 19th century, an English company made the first **solid** block of sweetened chocolate. Now people could both drink and eat chocolate. Later, a Swiss company mixed milk and chocolate together. People liked the taste of milk chocolate even better.

Besides the chocolate candy bar, one of the most popular American snacks is the chocolate-chip cookie. **Favorite** desserts are chocolate cream pie and, of course, an ice cream sundae with hot fudge sauce.

not sweet

at a time in the past

pour

very old

found out

not liquid or gas

a Vocabulary

Put the right word in each blank. The sentences are from the text.

dessert	snack	bitter	pour
once	valued	discovered	ancient
wealthy	solid	favorite	ingredient

1. Sometimes it's an _____ in the main course of a meal.

2. When the Spaniards took the drink back to Europe, people _____ that sugar removed the bitter taste of cacao.

3. For us, chocolate is a candy, but _____ it was a medicine.

4. The Mayas were an _____ people who once lived in Mexico.

5. In the 19th century, an English company made the first _____ block of sweetened chocolate.

6. _____ desserts are chocolate cream pie and, of course, an ice cream sundae with hot fudge sauce.

7. Mexicans make a hot chocolate sauce called *mole* and _____ it over chicken.

8. However, a long time ago, people thought of chocolate as something very _____.

9. They _____ the cacao tree.

10. Today, chocolate can be a hot drink, a frozen _____, or just a _____.

11. _____ Spaniards heated the sweet drink and thought that it was good for their health.

b Vocabulary: New Context

Put the right word in each blank.

values	snack	ingredient	once
discovered	favorite	wealthy	bitter
dessert	ancient	solid	pour

1. Mrs. Mendez said Pavarotti was her _____ singer. Her daughter chose Madonna.

2. The people who _____ lived here are now in Europe.

3. The coffee was so _____ that nobody wanted to drink it.

4. The Smiths _____ some dinosaur bones on their farm.

5. Would you please _____ some hot water into the cup?

6. I don't have anything sweet for _____, but we can have some fruit.

7. Most _____ civilizations had some kind of writing system.

8. He wasn't happy when he was poor, and he's not happy now that he is _____.

9. The family _____ the chair because it belonged to their grandfather.

10. I'm so hungry! And I didn't even bring a _____ with me!

11. The main _____ in that cake is chocolate.

12. The pond is frozen _____, so we can go skating.

c Vocabulary Review

Put the right word in each blank.

valleys	miss	experience	participated
order	forbidden	dairy	eliminate
ahead	throw	chemicals	on purpose

1. They have more than 100 cows at their _____ farm.

2. Fifty soccer players _____ in the tournament.

3. At this time of year, snow still covers the mountains and

   _____.

4. You might feel better if you _____ all dairy products from
   your meals.

5. Are there any _____ foods in your religion?

6. When I _____ the bus, I have to walk to school.

7. Did you _____ fish or meat?

8. That meat doesn't smell very good. I think you should

   _____ it away.

9. The trip was a great _____ for all the family except
   Grandma. She found the weather too hot.

10. Some _____ are poisonous.

11. He doesn't have any desserts in the house _____; he wants
    to lose weight.

12. What's that in the road _____? It looks like a cow.

d Comprehension: True/False/No Information

*Write T if the sentence is true. Write F if it is false. Write NI if no information about
the sentence was given in the text.*

_____ 1. The Spaniards arrived in Mexico in the 17th century.

_____ 2. Chocolate was always a dessert.

_____ 3. The Maya added sugar to chocolate and heated it.

_____ 4. The cacao tree grows in tropical countries.

_____ 5. Because chocolate was bitter, some people thought it was a medicine.

_____ 6. The Mayas lived in Argentina.

_____ 7. The Mayas used the cacao beans as hooks.

_____ 8. Hot chocolate was an expensive drink in Spain.

_____ 9. In the Philippines, people drink chocolate for breakfast.

_____10. Some people once believed that chocolate was good for your health.

_____11. Europeans produced the first solid blocks of sweet chocolate.

 e Questions

The asterisk (*) means you have to think of the answer. You cannot find it in the text.

1. Was chocolate once a medicine? What did it taste like?
*2. Does the cacao tree grow in Canada? Why or why not?
*3. Can you eat cacao beans? Why or why not?
4. Where does the word *chocolate* come from?
5. Who were the Mayas?
6. Where did they live?
*7. Why did the Mayas value the cacao tree?
8. What uses did they have for cacao beans?
9. When did the Spaniards come to Mexico?
10. How did the cacao bean get to Europe?
11. What did people add to chocolate to make it more popular?
12. What are some popular foods that use chocolate as an ingredient?

f Main Idea

Which is the main idea of this lesson? Choose one.

1. Over the years, people used chocolate in many different ways.
2. The Spaniards brought the cacao bean from Mexico to Europe.
3. Although chocolate comes from the tropics, you can buy it in cool climates.

lesson 4

The Blue Revolution

© David Samuel Robbins/CORBIS

Before You Read

1. How many times a month do you eat fish?

2. Where does your fish come from?

3. What do you know about fish farming?

97

4   The Blue Revolution

The **population** of the world is increasing **rapidly.** By 2020, there could be 7.5 billion people on earth. Will there be enough food for all these people, or will we have a food **shortage?** Some scientists think fish farming could solve this problem. However, other scientists **worry** that fish farming could cause serious environmental problems.

number of people in a place

very quickly

Fish farming is not a new thing. There were fish farms in China 3,000 years ago. Today, about one-third of the fish we eat comes from fish farms.

Most fish farms raise plant-eating fish. Popular kinds of plant-eating fish are carp, tilapia, and catfish. Unfortunately, many fish farms are starting to raise meat-eating fish. A popular type of meat-eating fish is salmon. These meat-eating fish live on **processed** food made from wild fish. However, it takes up to 5 tons of wild fish to produce just 1 ton of farm-raised salmon. The supply of wild fish is already **decreasing. Eventually,** many types of wild fish could become **extinct.** What will we do then?

going down

Critics of fish farming also say that farm-raised fish is unhealthy for **humans.** They say the fish contains dangerous chemicals. They also criticize fish farming because it pollutes the water. Another criticism is that farm-raised fish can spread diseases to wild fish.

people

Some people say that the farming **methods** being used now won't produce enough fish anyway. Instead of putting fish farms in lakes or near the coast, they say that the fish farms should be moved far out into the ocean. Several countries are already **experimenting** with deep-ocean farms. In the future, fish farms might be large **cages** that move across the ocean.

testing

boxes made of metal wire or bars

Like most things, there is both a good and a bad side to fish farming. Fish farming may help to feed millions of people. At the same time, however, fish farming may damage the environment.

98

a Vocabulary

Put the right word in each blank. The sentences are from the text.

population	eventually	cages	shortage
processed	methods	decreasing	rapidly
critics	extinct	humans	experimenting
worry			

1. Several countries are already _____ with deep-ocean farms.

2. _____, many types of wild fish could become
   _____.

3. Some people say that the farming _____ being used now
   won't produce enough fish anyway.

3. The supply of wild fish is already _____.

4. In the future, fish farms might be large _____ that move
   across the ocean.

5. The _____ of the world is increasing _____.

6. These meat-eating fish live on _____ food made from
   wild fish.

7. _____ of fish farming say that farm-raised fish is unhealthy
   for _____.

8. However, other scientists _____ that fish farming could
   cause serious environmental problems.

9. Will there be enough food for all these people, or will we have a food
   _____?

b Vocabulary: New Context

Put the right word in each blank.

eventually	method	processed	worry
population	shortage	humans	criticized
decrease	extinct	cage	experiment
rapid			

1. Soda and hot dogs are examples of _____ food.

2. Do you _____ more about your health or the environment's health?

3. _____ breathing can be a sign of a heart problem.

4. China has the largest _____ in the world.

5. My mother doesn't like to follow cooking recipes. She prefers to _____.

6. Why did dinosaurs become _____?

7. My teacher _____ me for coming to class late.

8. When an animal travels by airplane, it is kept in a _____.

9. If you _____ the amount of food you eat, you will lose weight.

10. I hope we _____ find solutions to our environmental problems.

11. Which cooking _____ do you prefer for fish—frying or baking?

12. _____ can't breath under water without special equipment.

13. The bad weather destroyed the crop of corn. Now there is a _____ of corn.

C Vocabulary Review

Match the word in Column A with the word or phrase in Column B that means the opposite. The first one is done for you.

Column A

1. solid _____*c. liquid*_____
2. scary _____
3. rare _____
4. powerful _____
5. bitter _____
6. forbid _____
7. double _____
8. recently _____
9. eliminate _____
10. wealthy _____

Column B

a. half
b. sweet
c. liquid
d. add
e. a long time ago
f. poor
g. common
h. funny
i. weak
j. allow

d Comprehension: Multiple Choice

Put a circle around the letter of the best answer.

1. The population of the world is increasing _____.
   a. slowly
   b. a little
   c. quickly
   d. rarely

2. Salmon is a type of _____ fish.
   a. dangerous
   b. extinct
   c. meat-eating
   d. plant-eating

3. Plant-eating fish are _____ than meat-eating fish.
   a. more expensive
   b. rarer
   c. better for the environment
   d. more dangerous

4. In the future, fish farms might be _____.
   a. less expensive
   b. easier to manage
   c. less polluting
   d. in deeper water

5. _____ of the fish we eat today comes from fish farms.
   a. Most
   b. More than half
   c. Between a quarter and a half
   d. Very little

6. Farm-raised fish _____ than wild fish.
   a. eat more processed food
   b. are more common
   c. need more food
   d. contain less chemicals

7. Carp and catfish eat _____.
   a. plants
   b. processed food
   c. less valuable fish
   d. shrimp

8. Critics of fish farming think that farm-raised fish is _____.
   a. healthy to eat
   b. dangerous for the environment
   c. processed too much
   d. too expensive for many people

 e Questions

The asterisk (*) means you have to think of the answer. You cannot find it in the text.

1. What is happening to the population of the world?
2. How much farm-raised fish do people eat now?
3. How is carp different from salmon?
*4. Why do you think fish farms existed in China thousands of years ago?
5. Why do some people criticize fish farming?
*6. Why might farmers feed chemicals to their fish?
*7. How could fish farming solve a future food shortage?
*8. Do you think fish farms should stop raising salmon? Why or why not?

 f Main Idea

Which is the main idea of this lesson? Choose one.

1. Fish farms can both help us and hurt us.
2. There will never be enough food for everyone.
3. Meat-eating fish contain more chemicals than plant-eating fish.

lesson

5

Twenty-One Days
Without Food

© Royalty-Free/CORBIS

Before You Read

1. *Fasting* means going without food on purpose. Why might
   someone fast?

2. Do you think it's unhealthy to fast?

3. Do you think fasting is dangerous?

5   Twenty-One Days Without Food

Why would someone decide to stop eating? We know that the body needs food in order to **function** well. However, many people fast at some time during their lives. Why is this?

Some people fast for **political** reasons. In the early 20th century, women in England and the United States weren't allowed to **vote.** In **protest**, many women went on fasts. They hoped that fasting would bring **attention** to this **injustice.** Mohandas Gandhi, the famous Indian leader, fasted 17 times during his life. For Gandhi, fasting was a powerful political tool. In 1943, he fasted to bring attention to his country's need for **independence.** For 21 days, he went without food. Another famous faster was Cesar Chavez. In the 1960s, he fasted for three weeks. Why? His goal was to bring attention to the terrible working **conditions** of farm workers in the United States.

Fasting is also a spiritual practice in many religions. Every year during the month of Ramadan, which is a religious holiday, Muslims fast from sunrise to sunset. Many Hindus fast on special **occasions,** as do some Christians and Buddhists.

Of course, not everyone fasts for political or religious reasons. Some people occasionally fast just because it makes them feel better. The American writer Mark Twain thought fasting was the best medicine for common **illnesses.** Whenever he had a cold or a fever, he stopped eating completely. He said that this always made his cold or fever go away. Another American writer, Upton Sinclair, discovered fasting after years of overeating, **indigestion**, and headaches. His first fast lasted for 12 days. During this time, his headaches and stomachaches went away. Sinclair said that fasting also made him more alert and energetic.

Choosing to go without food can be very dangerous. However, that doesn't stop people from fasting for political, religious, or health reasons.

work

anything that is unfair

freedom

sicknesses

stomachache caused by food

104

a   Vocabulary

Put the right word in each blank. The sentences are from the text.

function	political	vote	illnesses
protest	attention	injustice	independence
indigestion	conditions	occasions	

1. In the early 20th century, women in England and the United States weren't allowed to _____.

2. In 1943, he fasted to bring attention to his country's need for

   _____.

3. His goal was to bring attention to the terrible working

   _____ of farm workers in the United States.

4. Many Hindus fast on special _____, as do some Christians and Buddhists.

5. We know that the body needs food in order to _____ well.

6. In _____, many women went on fasts.

7. Some people fast for _____ reasons.

8. The American writer Mark Twain thought fasting was the best medicine for common _____.

9. Another American writer, Upton Sinclair, discovered fasting after years of overeating, _____, and headaches.

10. They hoped that fasting would bring _____ to this

    _____.

b   Vocabulary: New Context

Put the right word in each blank.

illness	attention	injustice	political
protested	condition	independent	occasion
function	vote	indigestion	

1. He bought a new television because his old one didn't _____ well.
2. Her friend was in the hospital for two weeks with a serious _____.
3. My aunt is a very _____ person. She doesn't want other people to do things for her.
4. I called his name, but I couldn't get his _____. He drove by without seeing me.
5. She can't drive her car long distances because it's in bad _____.
6. In the United States, there are two main _____ parties—Democratic and Republican.
7. Many foods can cause _____. Eating late at night can, too.
8. In the 1960s, many young Americans _____ against the war in Vietnam.
9. Every four years, people in the United States _____ for a president.
10. It's an _____ that some people are very wealthy, while others are very poor.
11. The birth of a child is an important _____.

c   Vocabulary Review

Underline the word that does not belong in each group.

1. dangerous, proud, risky, scary
2. experiment, try, test, pour
3. embarrassment, indigestion, headache, backache
4. protest, disagree, accept, criticize
5. think, worry, wonder, exercise
6. dessert, carpenter, snack, meal
7. elbow, knee, back, pray
8. human, engineer, carpenter, coach

106

d   Comprehension: True/False/No Information

Write T *if the sentence is true. Write* F *if it is false. Write* NI *if no information about the sentence was given in the text.*

_____ 1. Women in the United States got the right to vote in the early 20th century.

_____ 2. Mohandas Gandhi was a famous British leader.

_____ 3. One time, Gandhi went without food for twenty-one days.

_____ 4. Gandhi protested the independence of his country.

_____ 5. Cesar Chavez fasted for health reasons.

_____ 6. During Ramadan, Muslims fast during the day but not at night.

_____ 7. Sinclair Lewis wrote a book about fasting.

_____ 8. Mark Twain fasted when he felt sick.

_____ 9. Doctors say that fasting is good for you.

_____10. It's a fact that fasting is good for your body.

e   Questions

The asterisk (*) means you have to think of the answer. You cannot find it in the text.

  1. What is fasting?

*2. Why is fasting dangerous?

  3. What is an example of an injustice?

  4. Fasting is one way to protest. What are some other ways?

  5. Why did Gandhi fast at different times during his life?

  6. What do Gandhi and Chavez have in common?

  7. What do Twain and Sinclair have in common?

  8. Why did Sinclair go on fasts?

*9. Why else might someone fast?

f   Main Idea

Which is the main idea of this lesson? Choose one.

1. When you fast, you stop eating completely.
2. People go on fasts for many different reasons.
3. Many famous people fasted for political reasons.

Word Study

a | Count/Noncount Nouns

In English, nouns can be count nouns or noncount nouns. Count nouns have a singular form and a plural form. Noncount nouns have only a singular form. They do not have a plural form.

Examples:

Count Nouns

I had an unusual **experience** yesterday.
Her **experiences** in China were interesting.
A **customer** just came in the store.
There are three **customers** in the store.

Noncount Nouns

Don't forget to take your **money.**
Money is valuable.
The **rice** here is delicious.
There is a lot of **rice** on the table.

Use one of the following nouns to complete each sentence below.

Count Nouns

ingredient	ingredients
chemical	chemicals
customer	customers
foreigner	foreigners

Noncount Nouns

meat
population
water
money

1. Do you have all the _____ to make bread?
2. What is the _____ of Brazil?
3. How much _____ do you eat every week?
4. What are the most dangerous _____ in the world?
5. Is this _____ from a bottle?
6. Are there any _____ in your class?
7. How many _____ came into the store today?
8. Do you have any _____ in your wallet?

b | Adjectives with -able

Add the suffix -able to these verbs to form adjectives. Write the adjectives in the blanks.

Verb	**Adjective**	**Verb**	**Adjective**
accept	_____	train	_____
avoid	_____	pour	_____

Drop the final -e on these verbs, and then add the suffix -able. Write the adjectives in the blanks.

Verb	**Adjective**	**Verb**	**Adjective**
remove	_____	believe	_____
value	_____	use	_____
measure	_____		

Can you think of an example of each of these? Write a sentence using the example. The first one is done for you.

1. Something valuable   *Gold is valuable.*
2. Something unbelievable   _____
3. Something measurable   _____
4. Something usable in the kitchen   _____
5. Something enjoyable   _____

C Word Forms

Verb	Noun	Adjective
1. discover	discovery	(none)
2. risk	risk	risky
3. scare	scare	scary
4. vote	vote	(none)
5. experiment	experiment	experimental
6. avoid	avoidance	avoidable
7. criticize	critic, criticism	critical
8. value	value	valuable
9. (none)	medicine	medicinal

Put the correct word form in each blank. Use words from line 1 in item 1, and so on. Use the right verb forms and singular or plural nouns.

1. When she _____ the chemicals in the water, she was shocked. Her _____ angered everyone in town.

2. It's too _____ to climb that rock in the rain. It's all right to take a _____ sometimes, but that would be madness. I just can't _____ it.

3. We had a big _____ when the tree fell on the house. It was a _____ experience.

4. Only 50 percent of the population _____ this year. The new president got 75 percent of the _____.

5. My friend is in an _____ program for people with knee problems.

6. That accident was _____. I don't understand why he didn't try to _____ it.

7. My teacher was very _____ of my work, but his _____ was very helpful.

8. I'm sure your necklace is very _____. What _____ did the jeweler place on it? I'm sure you _____ it very highly.

9. The doctor prescribed a _____ drink. It tasted more like a soft drink than _____.

d   Past Tense Review

Write the past tense of each verb.

1. bury _____
2. scare _____
3. contain _____
4. value _____
5. discover _____
6. find out _____
7. double _____
8. experiment _____

9. miss _____
10. worry _____
11. decrease _____
12. pour _____
13. avoid _____
14. risk _____
15. take turns _____

e   Collocations

Some words are often used together. For example, we often use the word
bring *with the words* attention *and* to. *Read these groups of words.*
Use them in the sentences below.

    bring attention to   give your attention to   pay attention
    had their attention   get our attention

1. All of the employees decided to stop working. They hoped
   this would _____ the unsafe working
   conditions in the factory.
2. A loud bell rang to _____.
3. The teacher told the children an exciting story. He
   _____ for a whole hour.
4. She doesn't do very well in school because she can't
   _____ in class.
5. Would you please _____ the map on the wall?

f   Writing

Choose one or more of these topics and write answers.

1. What's your favorite food? Why do you like it?
2. What is a popular food to eat on a holiday in your country?
   Why is it so popular?
3. Not everyone in the world has a healthy diet. What are some
   of the reasons for this?

111

Video Highlights

a   Before You Watch

1. You've read about the puffer fish. Now read the five sentences below. Write T *if a sentence is true. Write* F *if it is not true.*

_____ a. The puffer fish is poisonous.

_____ b. The puffer fish can double itself in size.

_____ c. The puffer fish lives off the coast of Canada.

_____ d. The puffer fish is a popular food in Central America.

_____ e. The puffer fish is called *fugu* in Japanese.

2. These words will help you understand the video. Read the words and their definitions.

> **cyanide:** a deadly poison
> **gourmet:** an expert on fine food
> **licensed:** permitted by the government or an official group
> **antidote:** a cure for someone who ate a poison
> **auctioneer:** a person in charge of public sales

3. Choose one of the words above for each of these sentences.

a. She refused to eat at fast-food restaurants because she was a _____.

b. The _____ sold the house for $500,000.

c. That restaurant is _____ to sell alcohol.

d. The poison of the puffer fish is hundreds of times more deadly than _____.

e. There is an _____ for most poisonous snake bites, but none for the poison in a puffer fish.

b As You Watch

You will see five places in the video. In each place, people are doing different activities. As you watch, draw lines to connect the people with the places and the activities. One is done for you.

Places	People	Activities
fish market	chefs	put live puffer fish in trays
restaurant	cutters	arrange *fugu* on a plate
fish factory	buyers and sellers	eat *fugu*
auction	workers	put their hands under a cloth
restaurant kitchen	diners	remove insides of puffer fish

c After You Watch

1. The people who sell puffer fish say that no more than a dozen people die each year from eating it. But some journalists and other writers say that more than one hundred people die every year. What does the interviewer say on the video?

   _____

2. In the video, a puffer fish seller says he wants to export *fugu* to other countries. He says he will export *fugu* without its poisonous parts. Imagine that you are a buyer in another country. What questions would you ask him before buying his product?

   _____

   _____

   _____

   _____

3. Does the puffer fish seller have the right to export his fish? Take a vote in your class and see which opinion wins.

Activity Page

In a Restaurant

1. Nathan, Birgit, Shao Wong, and Chandra are ordering food in a restaurant. Read what they're saying about their likes and dislikes, then choose a meal for each person.

I can't eat dairy products.

I can't eat meat or fish.

I don't like eggs.

I love unusual foods.

Shao Wong   Chandra   Nathan   Birgit

Menu

Appetizers	**Soup**
Mixed Salad	*Shark Fin*
100-Year-Old Eggs	*Cheese and Onion*
Creamed Beef on Toast	*Beef and Noodle*
Cheese Puffs	*Egg and Sweet Corn*

Main Course	**Dessert**
Roast Beef with Vegetables	*Chocolate Cream Pie*
Fish with Cream Sauce	*Fresh Apricots*
Soyburger with Salad	*Cheese and Crackers*
Lobster Mayonnaise	*Ice-Cream Sundae*

	Shao Wong	Chandra	Nathan	Birgit
Appetizer	_____	_____	_____	_____
Soup	_____	_____	_____	_____
Main Course	_____	_____	_____	_____
Dessert	_____	_____	_____	_____

2. Pretend you're one of the four people in activity 1. Order a meal. Your partner has to guess which of the four people you are.

Example: For an appetizer, I'd like 100-Year-Old Eggs. Then I'll have Shark-Fin Soup. For my main course, I'm going to choose . . . . (Birgit)

Parts of Speech

1. The dictionary entries below contain the names of different parts of speech (noun, verb, adverb, and adjective). One is circled. Circle the others.

> **experience** /ɪkˈspɪriəns/ (noun)
> **1** an event: *Our visit to Alaska was a pleasant experience.*
> **2** understanding gained through doing something: *She has years of experience in teaching.*
> **experience** *verb* **experienced, experiencing, experiences**
> to feel or know by personal involvement in: *She has experienced difficulties (satisfaction, success, etc.) in her new job.*
>
> **populate** /ˈpapyəˌleɪt/ *verb* **populated, populating, populates**
> **1** to fill an area with people: *People from Europe populated many parts of the Americas.*
> **2** to live in an area, to inhabit it: *People from all over the world populate New York City.*
>
> **population** /ˌpapyəˈleɪʃən/ *noun*
> all of the people living in a specific area: *The population of this city is 8 million.*
>
> **rapid** /ˈræpɪd/ *adjective*
> very fast, quick: *His rapid speech is difficult to understand.* —*adverb* **rapidly.**

2. Choose a word from the entries above for each sentence below. Use the correct verb forms and singular or plural nouns.

a. He wrote about his many strange _____ while living in the desert.

b. There was a _____ increase in the price of gasoline last month.

c. Fifty percent of the _____ here travels to work by bus.

d. The fast train will take us _____ to London.

e. She _____ severe stomach pain after eating the leftover food.

3. *In the dictionary entries below, the parts of speech are missing. Read each entry carefully, and then write* noun, verb, adjective, *or* adverb *in the space provided.*

critical /ˈkrɪtɪkəl/ (_____)
1 pointing out problems: *The teacher wrote critical remarks on my paper about mistakes that I made.*
2 very important: *It is critical that you study for the exam or you will fail it.*
3 dangerous, urgent: *Her illness is at the critical stage where she may die.*

criticize /ˈkrɪtəˌsaɪz/ (_____)
critcized, criticizing, criticizes
1 to evaluate some form of art as a profession: *The newspaper's critic criticized the new movie as boring.*
2 to point out faults in someone or something: *The teacher criticized the student's poor spelling.*

valuable /ˈvælyuəbəl, -yəbəl/
(_____)
1 having worth or value: *Gold jewelry is valuable.*
2 useful, helpful: *a valuable piece of information*

valuables (_____)
objects that have a high monetary value such as jewelry or artwork: *She keeps her valuables in a safe.*

value /ˈvælyu/ (_____)
valued, valuing, values
1 to think something is important: *I value my best friend's advice.*
2 to put a price on something: *An expert valued the painting at $1 million.*

value (_____)
1 worth: *The value of this home has doubled since we have owned it.*
2 *plural* ideals, standards: *We have tried to teach our children values like honesty and hard work.*

Mysteries

Context Clues

Put a circle around the letter of the answer that means the same as the word in bold.

1. At midnight there was a loud noise in the kitchen. Ali went to the kitchen, but no one was there. The cause of the noise was a **mystery.**
   a. something pleasant
   b. something normal
   c. something familiar
   d. something unknown

2. Juan couldn't find anyone at school when he got there. The school was **deserted.**
   a. closed for the day
   b. without any people
   c. dark
   d. full of people

3. Yuri opened his **diary** and turned to a new page. What had happened that day? He thought for a few minutes and then began to write.
   a. record of the day's events
   b. list of daily tasks
   c. newspaper
   d. shopping list

4. We could see the **tracks** of a large animal in the snow.
   a. ears
   b. footprints
   c. elbows
   d. hooks

5. Sara writes stories and poems about the future. She has a wonderful **imagination.**
   a. knowledge
   b. creative ability
   c. mental ability
   d. mathematical ability

6. Lori didn't come to class yesterday, but the teacher didn't notice that she was **absent.**
   a. sick
   b. careless
   c. not serious
   d. not there

7. That island is very **isolated.** The nearest land is hundreds of miles away.
   a. near other places
   c. far from other places
   b. deserted
   d. pleasant

8. Most of the Europeans who came to America in the early days **settled** along the northeast coast. Only a few people moved south.
   a. looked at the land
   c. explored
   b. moved in and stayed
   d. relocated

9. Three **generations** live in my house—me, my parents, and my grandparents.
   a. families
   b. age levels in a family
   c. committees
   d. important events in a day

10. You hear a loud noise when something in the distance **explodes.**
   a. goes away slowly
   b. becomes rare
   c. blows apart forcefully
   d. moves on the floor

11. Someone put a fence around the garden to **prevent** animals from entering.
   a. stop
   c. help
   b. allow
   d. encourage

The Marie Celeste

© Hulton Archive/getty images

Before You Read

1. What are the names of some famous ships?

2. What might happen to a ship when it goes across the ocean?

3. Do you like to read mysteries?

1　The Marie Celeste

There are many stories about the ocean. One of the strangest is a true story about a sailing ship. It is a **mystery** even today.

In 1872, the *Marie Celeste* started on a trip across the Atlantic Ocean with a **crew** of ten people. Some time later, the captain of another ship, the *Dei Gratia*, saw the *Marie Celeste*. There was something strange about its **appearance.** The captain called out, but there was no answer. The *Marie Celeste* seemed **deserted.**

When the captain went to **inspect** the ship, no one came to meet him. He knew something was wrong, but there were no signs of **violence.** Nothing was missing, and there was no **damage** to the ship's instruments. And strangely enough, there was food on the table. Where was everyone? Did the crew jump from the *Marie Celeste*? Or did something come up from the ocean and take the captain and crew away?

The captain of the *Dei Gratia* looked around for **clues.** The last entry in the *Marie Celeste's* **diary** was ten days earlier. However, the food on the table was only a few days old. Someone was on the ship a few days before, but they didn't write anything in the ship's diary. Why?

There were many different **explanations** for the mystery of the *Marie Celeste*. Some people thought that a **huge** octopus ate the crew. Others said bad weather carried them away. A few people believed that the *Marie Celeste* was under a **curse,** because it **sank** on a later voyage. Now that the *Marie Celeste* lies somewhere at the bottom of the ocean, no one can ever solve the mystery.

crew

empty

look at carefully

very large

went underwater

a Vocabulary

Put the right word in each blank. The sentences are from the text.

crew	diary	appearance	huge
clues	inspect	curse	
explanations	mystery	sank	
deserted	damage	violence	

1. Nothing was missing, and there was no _____ to the ship's instruments.

2. A few people believed that the *Marie Celeste* was under a _____, because it _____ on a later voyage.

3. The *Marie Celeste* seemed _____.

4. In 1872, the *Marie Celeste* started on a trip across the Atlantic Ocean with a _____ of ten people.

5. When the captain went to _____ the ship, no one came to meet him.

6. There were many different _____ for the mystery of the *Marie Celeste*.

7. He knew something was wrong, but there were no signs of _____.

8. It is a _____ even today.

9. There was something strange about its _____.

10. The last entry in the *Marie Celeste's* _____ was ten days earlier.

11. The captain of the *Dei Gratia* looked around for _____.

12. Some people thought that a _____ octopus ate the crew.

Put the right word in each blank.

curse	diary	huge	appeared
clues	explanation	mystery	damage
violently	deserted	inspect	sank
crew			

1. He looked at the _____ to his car. It was worse than he thought.
2. The captain and _____ were happy the voyage was over.
3. A strong wind shook the boat _____.
4. Many young people keep a _____ in which they write down all their secrets.
5. An officer came to _____ the burned house. He reported that the fire was an accident.
6. Although the house seemed _____, Sally was sure someone lived there.
7. He was late for class, but he had a good _____.
8. I threw a coin in the water, and it quickly _____.
9. It was a _____. Someone entered a locked room and took the money.
10. They live in a _____ house. It has more than 30 rooms.
11. The only _____ to the murder were a train ticket and a key.
12. That family seems to be under a _____. Three of their children died in less than a year.
13. When the president _____, everyone in the room stood up.

c Vocabulary Review

Put the right word in each blank.

processed	retired	customers	leak
ingredients	steps	took place	career
eventually	except	risky	shortage

1. Everyone is going to the tournament _____ my brother. He is going to stay at home.

2. In the morning, the store is usually empty, but in the afternoon there are usually a lot of _____.

3. A lot of _____ foods come in cans.

4. Their son took his first few _____ yesterday.

5. Do you know when the American Revolution _____?

6. If she works hard, she will _____ become a great athlete.

7. My uncle was very bored after he _____, so he got a part-time job.

8. It's very _____ to ride in a car without wearing your seatbelt.

9. When there is a _____ of something, the price usually goes up.

10. One of the _____ in my favorite food is salt.

11. He hopes to have a _____ in medicine, but he doesn't want to work in a hospital.

12. A lot of water came into the house through a _____ in the roof.

d Comprehension: Multiple Choice

Put a circle around the letter of the best answer.

1. The name of the ship that disappeared was _____.
   a. the *Dei Gratia*   b. a mystery   c. the *Marie Celeste*   d. the *Marie Azores*

2. The *Marie Celeste* was sailing in the _____ Ocean.
   a. Atlantic   b. Indian   c. Pacific   d. Japanese

3. The story takes place in the year _____.
   a. The year is not given.   b. 1880   c. 1782   d. 1872

4. The captain who discovered the *Marie Celeste* was called _____.
   a. Michael
   b. The captain's name is not given.
   c. Captain Nicolai
   d. Dei Gratia

5. There was a _____ on the table.
   a. fight   b. death   c. storm   d. meal

6. The last entry in the diary was _____ days before.
   a. four   b. seven   c. 400   d. ten

7. The food on the table was only _____ old.
   a. a few hours   b. seven days   c. a few days   d. some days

8. The mystery of the *Marie Celeste* was _____ solved.
   a. probably   b. never   c. finally   d. at last

e   Questions

The asterisk (*) means you have to think of the answer. You cannot find it in the text.

   1. What kind of a ship was the *Marie Celeste*?
   2. How many crew members were on the *Marie Celeste* at the beginning of the trip? How many when she was discovered?
   3. Where was the ship going?
   4. Did this take place less than a century ago? More than a century ago? What was the date?
   5. Who first knew something was wrong with the *Marie Celeste*?
   6. Why did the captain go to inspect the *Marie Celeste*?
   7. When was the last entry in the ship's diary? When was the last meal eaten?
   *8. What is strange about these last two facts?
   9. Was anyone able to explain the mystery of the *Marie Celeste*?
   *10. What do you think happened to the crew of the *Marie Celeste*?
   11. What happened to the *Marie Celeste* on a later voyage?

f   Main Idea

Which is the main idea of this lesson? Choose one.

1. No one can explain what happened to the captain and crew of the *Marie Celeste*.
2. There are many strange things in the ocean, and that's why it's dangerous to travel by ship.
3. The *Marie Celeste* traveled across the Atlantic Ocean without a captain and crew.

lesson 2   The Roanoke Settlement

© CORBIS

Before You Read

1. What does the picture show that tells you the man is an explorer?

2. What do you know about the first Europeans who came to live in North America?

3. What new places have you explored?

2 The Roanoke Settlement

Only a few Europeans lived in North America in the 16th century. Most of them **settled** on the northeast coast. In 1587, a small group of about 100 people decided to go south. They moved to the small island of Roanoke. That area later became part of the state of North Carolina.

stayed to live

Unfortunately, the Roanoke settlers weren't well prepared. They didn't have enough food for the winter, and there wasn't enough grain for future crops. Their leader, Captain White, decided to sail back to England to get supplies. However, there was a **war** in Europe, and three years passed before he returned to North America.

When Captain White came back to Roanoke in 1590, he was **eager** to see the settlers. He looked out from his ship, but no one was there to meet him. There were no signs of life. The settlement was deserted.

No one knows why the Roanoke settlers **disappeared.** Many people thought that **hostile** Native Americans killed them, but there were no signs of a **fight.** Some thought that the settlers died from hunger or disease, but they couldn't explain the **absence** of bodies.

very unfriendly

Many years later, more settlers came to North Carolina. One of them met a Native American group called the Lumbee. They were unusual looking **compared** to the black-haired, brown-eyed Native Americans in the north. Some Lumbee had blonde hair and gray eyes. Then he listened to their speech and almost fell off his horse. They seemed to speak an **odd** kind of English!

unusual

He asked where they were from. None of them knew, but they said that their grandparents "talked from a book." Did they mean that their grandparents were able to read? As he rode back home, he asked himself a

question: Were the Lumbee people the **descendants** of
the Roanoke settlers?

   People are still asking the **identical** question.   same
Because there are no written records, we can't be certain.
However, there is one interesting fact. Today, some of
the Lumbee people have names like Sampson, Dare, and
Cooper. They are identical to the names of the **vanished**   disappeared
settlers of Roanoke Island.

a | Vocabulary

Put the right word in each blank. The sentences are from the text.

eager	vanished	settled
identical	fight	disappeared
descendants	compared	hostile
war	odd	absence

1. However, there was a _____ in Europe, and three years
   passed before he returned to North America.

2. No one knows why the Roanoke settlers _____.

3. Most of them _____ on the northeast coast.

4. They were unusual looking _____ to the black-haired,
   brown-eyed Native Americans in the north.

5. Some thought that the settlers died from hunger or disease, but they
   couldn't explain the _____ of bodies.

6. Were the Lumbee people the _____ of the
   Roanoke settlers?

7. They are _____ to the names of the _____
   settlers of Roanoke Island.

8. When Captain White came back to Roanoke in 1590, he was
   _____ to see the settlers.

9. Many people thought that _____ Native Americans killed
   them, but there were no signs of a _____.

10. They seemed to speak an _____ kind
    of English!

b Vocabulary: New Context

Put the right word in each blank.

eager	war	odd
settled	fighting	vanished
descendants	disappearance	absence
identical	compared	hostile

1. The _____ between the North and the South in the United States started in 1861.

2. There is an _____ smell in the house. I can't say what it is.

3. Most of the guests _____ after supper. I think they only came for the food.

4. _____ to last year, he is doing well in school.

5. During the revolution, there was a lot of _____.

6. Scientists are worried about the _____ of many types of animals.

7. Of course, the two girls look the same. They're _____ twins.

8. The Hansens live in that house. They are the _____ of the people who first came to our town 100 years ago.

9. Most of the first Eastern European immigrants to the United States _____ in big cities.

10. "I'm _____ to hear what you did in my _____," said Jenny. "Did you finish your book while I was away?"

11. At first, the tribes were friendly, but later they became _____.

c | Vocabulary Review

Match the word in Column A with the word in Column B that means the same. The first one is done for you.

Column A

1. immediately   *c. right now*
2. rapid   _____
3. quite a few   _____
4. explanation   _____
5. frequently   _____
6. powerful   _____
7. ahead   _____
8. ancient   _____
9. familiar   _____
10. bitter   _____

Column B

a. reason
b. often
c. right now
d. very old
e. not sweet
f. common
g. fast
h. many
i. in front
j. strong

d | Comprehension: Multiple Choice

Put a circle around the letter of the best answer.

1. When Captain White returned to the Roanoke settlement, _____ came to meet him.
   a. a tribe of Native Americans   c. a small group
   b. only one person   d. nobody

2. Only a few Europeans lived in North America in the _____.
   a. winter   c. Civil War years
   b. 16th century   d. 17th century

3. The Roanoke settlers _____ supplies for the winter.
   a. had enough   c. didn't have enough
   b. had plenty of   d. didn't need

4. Captain White stayed in England for _____.
   a. five years   c. three years
   b. five months   d. a few months

5. The Lumbee people spoke an odd kind of _____.
   a. English   c. French
   b. Native American language   d. Spanish

6. A group of about 100 people moved south to what is now the state of _____.
   a. South Carolina b. Virginia c. West Virginia d. North Carolina
7. Captain White didn't return to Roanoke for three years because there was a _____ in Europe.
   a. contest b. war c. revolution d. committee
8. Many years later, more settlers moved south and met a group of Native Americans called the _____.
   a. Roanokes b. Carolinas c. Lumbee d. Europeans
9. Some of the Lumbee names were _____ to those of the vanished Roanoke settlers.
   a. unknown b. identical c. unfamiliar d. odd

e Questions

The asterisk (*) means you have to think of the answer. You cannot find it in the text.

1. At first, where did most Europeans settle in North America?
2. How many people were in the group that moved south?
3. Where did they settle?
*4. Why were they called the Roanoke settlers?
5. Were the Roanoke settlers well prepared for winter?
6. Who decided to go back to England? Why?
7. How long was he away? What stopped him from coming back?
8. In what year did he come back? What did he see?
9. What was the name of the group of Native Americans who spoke an odd sort of English?
10. The Lumbee said that their grandparents "talked from a book." What is another way of saying this?
11. What are the names of some of the Lumbee people? What is interesting about those names?

f Main Idea

Which is the main idea of this lesson? Choose one.

1. In the late 16th century, the Roanoke settlers vanished, and no one knows where they went.
2. The Lumbee people are definitely descendants of the lost Roanoke settlers.
3. The mystery of the Roanoke settlement proves that the early European settlers in North America had a very difficult life.

The Easter Island Statues

© Wolfgang Kaehler/CORBIS

Before You Read

1. What are the statues in the picture probably made of?

2. How tall do you think they are?

3. Why do you think the statues are there?

3   The Easter Island Statues

When the first sailing ship came to Easter Island in 1722, the captain and crew were afraid to land. They saw **giants** looking down at them from the high **cliffs.** The giants didn't move, so the ship slowly moved closer. Finally, the sailors **realized** that the giants were **statues.** Who made these huge statues? How did they get there?

cliff
very large people or things

Easter Island is a very small island in the Pacific Ocean. It is more than 2,000 miles from the nearest continent (South America). It is one of the most **isolated** places on earth.

statues
away from other places and people

The biggest statue on Easter Island is over 60 feet high and weighs over 100 tons. There are hundreds of smaller ones, about 15 feet high. All of the statues are made of stone, and some wear stone hats. Their faces are **solemn** and unsmiling.

Earlier **inhabitants** of Easter Island made the statues from the rocks in a volcanic **crater.** Next, they had to move the statues a long distance. In some cases, they moved the statues to **locations** more than ten miles away.

people living in a place

places

No one knows for certain how the inhabitants were able to move the statues. Some scientists say that palm trees grew on Easter Island in the past. They think the inhabitants cut the trees down and placed the heavy statues on the trees. Then groups of 70 or more people **rolled** the statues to their **present** locations. Other scientists disagree with this **theory** because there are no palm trees on the island today. More important, the purpose of the statues is still a mystery. Was the purpose of the statues to **prevent** strangers from landing on the island?

crater
turned over and over

not allow

The result, however, has been the opposite. Large groups of eager people come to look at the statues. Easter Island now has a modern airport, and people come from all over the world to visit.

? 133

a Vocabulary

Put the right word in each blank. The sentences are from the text.

statues	cliffs	present	rolled
giants	locations	prevent	
theory	realized	isolated	
crater	inhabitants	solemn	

1. Their faces are _____ and unsmiling.

2. Finally, the sailors _____ that the giants were
   _____.

3. It is one of the most _____ places on earth.

4. They saw _____ looking down at them from the high
   _____.

5. In some cases, they moved the statues to _____ more than
   ten miles away.

6. Other scientists disagree with this _____ because there are
   no palm trees on the island today.

7. Earlier _____ of Easter Island made the statues from the
   rocks in a volcanic _____.

8. Then groups of 70 or more people _____ the statues to their
   _____ locations.

9. Was the purpose of the statues to _____ strangers from
   landing on the island?

b Vocabulary: New Context

Put the right word in each blank.

cliff	presently	roll	giant
isolation	location	inhabitants	theory
crater	realize	prevent	statues
solemn			

1. Don't carry the rock. Just _____ it down the hill.
2. In _____, we should get eight hours of sleep every night. In practice, we often sleep only five or six hours.
3. _____ of former kings and queens lined the entrance to the cathedral.
4. Last year, there were ten people in the club. _____, there are only five.
5. The redwood tree is a _____. It grows very tall.
6. Don't go too close to the side of the _____. You might fall off.
7. When did you _____ that your daughter is a good athlete?
8. One hundred years ago, the _____ of our town were all farmers.
9. The _____ of the volcano wasn't dead. The villagers expected it to erupt at any moment.
10. This is a very good _____ for our farm. It has water and lots of trees.
11. My grandfather was a _____ person. He almost never laughed.
12. What can we do to _____ the birds from returning and eating the fruit?
13. They put him in _____ because he had a contagious disease.

c Vocabulary Review

Match the word in Column A with the word in Column B that means the opposite.
The first one is done for you.

Column A   **Column B**

1. identical   *h. different*   a. presence

2. huge   _____   b. friendly

3. sinks   _____   c. very bad

4. hostile   _____   d. emptied

5. absence   _____   e. a long time ago

6. normal   _____   f. careful

7. excellent   _____   g. allows

8. careless   _____   h. different

9. filled   _____   i. refuse

10. decrease   _____   j. small

11. forbids   _____   k. unusual

12. strange   _____   l. familiar

13. recently   _____   m. increase

14. accept   _____   n. comes up

d Comprehension: True/False/No Information

Write T if the sentence is true. Write F if it is false. Write NI if no information about the sentence was given in the text.

_____ 1. The first ship to arrive at Easter Island was a steam ship.

_____ 2. At first, the sailors thought the giants were real people.

_____ 3. The sailors realized that the giants were statues.

_____ 4. Easter Island is very close to South America.

_____ 5. Easter Island lies in the Pacific Ocean.

_____ 6. There are many huge stone statues on the island.

_____ 7. The statues have smiling faces.

_____ 8. The present inhabitants of Easter Island made the statues.

_____ 9. There are many volcanoes on the island.

_____ 10. No palm trees grow on the island today.

_____ 11. The statues were placed on the cliffs to welcome visitors.

_____ 12. Today, many people visit Easter Island to look at the statues.

 Questions

The asterisk (*) means you have to think of the answer. You cannot find it in the text.

1. Is Easter Island large or small?
2. Which ocean is it in?
3. How far away is the nearest continent?
4. What are the statues on Easter Island made from?
5. How tall is the biggest statue?
6. How much does it weigh?
7. Can you describe the faces of the statues?
8. Where did the rocks for the statues come from?
9. How far did the inhabitants move some of the statues?
10. Did the present inhabitants of Easter Island make the statues?
11. What is one possible purpose of the statues?
*12. What do you think the purpose of the statues was?

f Main Idea

Which is the main idea of this lesson? Choose one.

1. The early inhabitants of Easter Island made huge statues whose purpose is a mystery.
2. The early inhabitants of Easter Island spent years placing the statues in their present locations.
3. Easter Island has many visitors every year.

lesson

4

The Tunguska Fireball

© The Image Bank/getty images

Before You Read

1. What is happening in the picture?

2. Where do meteors come from?

3. What other things come from space?

4   The Tunguska Fireball

plateau

The Tunguska **plateau** is an isolated area in central Siberia. On the morning of June 30, 1908, inhabitants of the area saw and heard a mysterious **explosion.** Fire **covered** the sky, and the earth **shook** violently. In the following nights, there were strange lights in the sky. The night sky was so **bright** that people could read the newspaper outdoors. Far away in Europe, many people <u>reported</u> seeing unusual lights in the night sky.

described

The Tunguska plateau is very difficult to reach, so no one went to inspect the <u>site</u> of the explosion. Most people thought the explosion was probably an earthquake, and they soon forgot about it.

place

Nineteen years passed before Leonid Kulik, a Russian scientist, went to look for the site of the explosion. With great difficulty, he traveled on foot to the Tunguska plateau. What he saw there amazed him. As far as he could see, the trees were black. Many lay **flat** on the **ground.** The explosion burned perhaps 80 million trees over an area of about 1,000 square miles. After seeing the destruction, Kulik decided that a <u>meteor</u> probably caused the explosion.

meteor

For many years, the meteor theory was the most popular explanation for the Tunguska explosion. However, there were problems with this theory. No one could find the crater where the meteor hit the ground, and no one could find any pieces of a meteor. <u>**In addition,**</u> some of the trees at the center of the explosion weren't burned.

also, besides

Over the years, there were many explanations for the Tunguska explosion. Some people thought it was a huge bomb. Others <u>suggested</u> that it was an exploding spaceship. One recent theory is that the meteor exploded in the air before it hit the ground. That explains the missing crater, but it doesn't explain the missing pieces of a meteor. A more recent theory

offered an idea

? _139_

suggests something completely different. Perhaps it wasn't something from outer space that destroyed the area. Instead, some scientists now think gas from the center of the earth caused the explosion.

Scientists continue to travel to the Tunguska plateau looking for clues to the cause of the explosion. Every few years newspapers report that scientists finally have a solution to the Tunguska mystery. **So far,** however, scientists can't agree on the cause of the explosion. For them, the Tunguska explosion is still one of the great mysteries of all time.

until now

a Vocabulary

Put the right word in each blank. The sentences are from the text.

bright	meteor	flat	plateau
site	covered	shook	suggested
in addition	so far	explosion	ground
reported			

1. Far away in Europe, many people _____ seeing unusual lights in the night sky.

2. Fire _____ the sky, and the earth _____ violently.

3. After seeing the destruction, Kulik decided that a _____ probably caused the explosion.

4. On the morning of June 30, 1908, inhabitants of the area saw and heard a mysterious _____.

5. Many lay _____ on the _____.

6. _____, however, scientists can't agree on the cause of the explosion.

7. The Tunguska plateau is very difficult to reach, so no one went to inspect the _____ of the explosion.

8. The night sky was so _____ that people could read the newspaper outdoors.

9. The Tunguska _____ is an isolated area in central Siberia.

10. Others _____ that it was an exploding spaceship.

11. _____, some of the trees at the center of the explosion weren't burned.

b Vocabulary: New Context

Put the right word in each blank.

bright	exploded	flat	suggestions
plateau	site	covered	shaking
in addition	so far	ground	meteor
reporter			

1. We are saving money to buy a car. _____, we have $2,000 in the bank.

2. The sun was so _____ that she had to wear sunglasses.

3. I looked up at the night sky, and suddenly a _____ flashed past.

4. _____ to soccer, he likes to play baseball and basketball.

5. We _____ the food on the table so that the flies couldn't touch it.

6. I dropped my watch on the _____, and now I can't find it.

7. I sat on his hat, and now it's _____.

8. The _____ of the battle is a museum. Many visitors go there every year.

9. What should we do this weekend? Do you have any _____?

10. He's so nervous that his hands are _____.

11. The _____ is high, over 3,000 feet above sea level.

12. The newspaper _____ inspected the site of the car accident and described what he saw.

13. After the car rolled over, it caught fire and _____.

c Vocabulary Review

Underline the word that does not belong in each group.

1. mysterious, odd, powerful, strange
2. inspect, vanish, disappear, go away
3. theory, idea, location, suggestion
4. location, flat, site, place
5. inhabitants, customers, crew, statues
6. meteor, plateau, valley, cliff
7. roll, curse, throw, touch
8. flat, bitter, sweet, delicious

d Comprehension: Multiple Choice

Put a circle around the letter of the best answer.

1. On June 30, 1908, there was a huge _____ in central Siberia.
   - a. damage
   - b. tundra
   - c. explosion
   - d. mystery

2. In 1908, the Tunguska plateau was _____.
   - a. very crowded
   - b. near a big city
   - c. a popular place to visit
   - d. far from everything

3. A plateau is _____.
   - a. an area destroyed by an explosion
   - b. a high flat area
   - c. a Siberian house
   - d. a bright light

4. No one inspected the site of the explosion in 1908 because _____.
   - a. it was hard to get to
   - b. it was dark at night
   - c. no one was interested
   - d. everyone thought the explosion was an earthquake

5. The Tunguska explosion burned _____.
   - a. everything in the area
   - b. most but not all trees in the area
   - c. all of the buildings in the area
   - d. a few trees in the area

6. At first, people thought _____ caused the explosion.
   a. gas   c. an earthquake
   b. a meteor   d. a spaceship

7. A meteor isn't a good explanation for the explosion because _____.
   a. there is no crater in the ground
   b. there aren't any pieces of a meteor in the area
   c. trees in the center of the area weren't burned
   d. all of the above

8. Today most scientists _____.
   a. don't agree on the cause of the explosion
   b. think that a meteor caused the explosion
   c. aren't interested in the cause of explosion
   d. think that a volcano caused the explosion

e Questions

The asterisk (*) means you have to think of the answer. You cannot find it in the text.

   1. Where is the Tunguska plateau?
   2. What happened there in 1908?
   3. How did people in Europe know that something happened there?
  *4. What usually happens when large meteors hit the earth?
   5. Why was it so long before any scientist traveled to the Tunguska plateau to see what had happened?
   6. What was the area like after nineteen years?
   7. Can you give two explanations for the Tunguska explosion?
   8. What's the problem with the meteor theory?
   9. What is the most recent explanation for the explosion?
 *10. What do you think caused the Tunguska explosion?

f Main Idea

Which is the main idea of this lesson? Choose one.

1. The Tunguska explosion in 1908 destroyed a huge area in central Siberia.
2. The Tunguska explosion was so powerful that people in Europe heard it.
3. In 1908, a mysterious explosion occurred in Siberia. No one really knows what happened.

Mystery of the Monarchs

© Dan Guravich/CORBIS

Before You Read

1. What do you know about butterflies?

2. How far do you think a butterfly can fly?

3. Can you think of anything mysterious about butterflies?

5   Mystery of the Monarchs

Monarch butterflies from the eastern part of North America make the most amazing **journey** in the insect world. Each year, this **tiny** creature travels up to 3,000 miles (4,800 kilometers) to its winter home in central Mexico. How can it fly so far? And what is the purpose of its long and dangerous trip? Scientists still don't have an explanation.

long trip
very small

For many years, people in Mexico **wondered** where the orange-and-black butterflies came from every winter. Then, in 1937, a scientist put the first wing **tags** on some of the butterflies. For the next 20 years, he tagged and **tracked** Monarch butterflies. He discovered that one butterfly started its journey in Ontario, Canada. Four months and 1,870 miles later, it arrived in Mexico.

asked themselves

tag

The length of the butterflies' trip is only one part of the mystery. Another amazing thing is that the butterflies always return to the same location in central Mexico. In fact, Monarchs from all over the eastern part of North America spend the winter at just a dozen places in Mexico. All of these places are within 300 square miles of each other! You can **imagine** how crowded the area is with butterflies.

How do the butterflies find their way back to the same place? This is an interesting question because only every fourth **generation** makes the trip south. In other words, the butterfly that travels to Mexico this year is the great-great-grandchild of the butterfly that traveled there last year.

Each year, four generations of a Monarch butterfly family are born. Each generation of the family has a very different life. The first generation of Monarchs is born in the south in late April. It slowly moves north, **reproduces,** and then dies. On the trip north, two more generations are born, reproduce, and die. Each of these generations of butterflies lives for only two to five weeks.

lays eggs or has babies

In the fall, the fourth generation of butterflies is born. Compared to its parents, this generation has a long life. It lives for about eight months. This generation of butterflies makes the amazing journey to the winter home of its great-great-grandparents. The butterflies spend the winter there, and in the spring they reproduce and then die. Their **offspring** will be the first generation   children
of the next **cycle.**

Today, people are still studying the Monarch butterfly. In 1997, **volunteers** tagged more than 75,000 butterflies. You can volunteer to help, too. Just go to the Internet and look up the organization Monarch Watch.

a | Vocabulary

Put the right word in each blank. The sentences are from the text.

offspring	tiny	wondered	tags
journey	volunteers	imagine	cycle
reproduces	generation	tracked	

1. For many years, people in Mexico _____ where the orange-and-black butterflies came from every winter.

2. It slowly moves north, _____, and then dies.

3. Monarch butterflies from the eastern part of North America make the most amazing _____ in the insect world.

4. In 1997, _____ tagged more than 75,000 butterflies.

5. Each year, this _____ creature travels up to 3,000 miles (4,800 kilometers) to its winter home in central Mexico.

6. For the next 20 years, he tagged and _____ Monarch butterflies.

7. This is an interesting question because only every fourth _____ makes the trip south.

8. Then, in 1937, a scientist put the first wing _____ on some of the butterflies.

9. Their _____ will be the first generation of the next _____.

10. You can _____ how crowded the area is with butterflies.

b Vocabulary: New Context

Put the right word in each blank.

offspring	tinier	journey	wonder
volunteer	imagine	tag	generations
reproduce	cycle	track	

1. Three _____ of my family live in the same house.

2. I put a _____ on my suitcase so that I could identify it at the airport.

3. I never saw a Monarch butterfly, but I can _____ what it looks like.

4. It's illegal to _____ a dollar bill.

5. She had to stop her _____ work because she needed to earn some money.

6. It's easy to _____ animals when there is snow on the ground.

7. This place is deserted. I _____ where everyone is.

8. Their _____ across the continent took several years.

9. I know your parents have at least one _____.

10. A poppy seed is _____ than an apple seed.

11. The _____ of the seasons is fall, winter, spring, and summer.

c   Vocabulary Review

Put the right word in each blank.

damage	descendents	encouraged	explain
inspect	diary	remove	missed
realize	eager	event	snack

1. My children and my grandchildren are my _____.
2. I left my notebook at school, but I didn't _____ it until I got home.
3. He did a lot of _____ to his car when he hit the tree.
4. She has a good record of her vacation because she wrote in her _____ almost every day.
5. I didn't want to participate in the event, but my parents _____ me to go.
6. Be sure to _____ the car carefully before you buy it.
7   I don't understand this definition. Could you _____ it to me?
8. I often have some fruit for a _____ in the middle of the afternoon.
9. The birth of a child is a happy _____ in a person's life.
10. When he was away, he _____ his friends and family a lot.
11. Do you usually _____ your shoes before you go inside?
12. They weren't _____ to come to the meeting, but they came anyway.

d   Comprehension: True/False/No Information

Write T if the sentence is true. Write F if it is false. Write NI if no information about the sentence was given in the text.

_____ 1. Eastern Monarch butterflies travel to Mexico for the winter.

_____ 2. All of the butterflies live in the same area during the summer.

_____ 3. Monarch butterflies travel all the way to Mexico without stopping.

_____ 4. The eastern Monarch butterflies live in different parts of Mexico.

_____ 5. Each generation lives for eight months.

_____ 6. The same butterfly makes the trip south to Mexico and then back north to Canada.

_____ 7. Monarch butterflies are orange and black.

_____ 8. In 1937, a scientist discovered why the butterflies make this long trip.

_____ 9. People are still tracking Monarch butterflies.

_____10. Scientists don't know why the butterflies always return to the same place.

_____11. The Monarch butterfly can fly very fast.

_____12. Three generations of butterflies live for just two to five weeks each.

Questions

The asterisk (*) means you have to think of the answer. You cannot find it in the text.

1. What does a Monarch butterfly look like?
2. Where does it go in the winter?
*3. Where does it live the rest of the year?
*4. How many miles a day can a butterfly fly?
5. How is the fourth generation of a Monarch family different from the other generations?
6. What is unusual about the Monarch butterflies' journey to Mexico?
7. How long does it take for a butterfly to reproduce?
*8. Why do you think people volunteer to tag butterflies?
*9. Do you think these insects are interesting?

f Main Idea

Which is the main idea of this lesson? Choose one.

1. It's a mystery how and why the Monarch butterfly returns to Mexico every year.
2. The eastern Monarch butterfly makes the longest journey of any insect in the world.
3. Each generation of Monarch butterflies lives a very different life from the others.

Word Study

a Conjunctions: *and/but*

We use conjunctions to connect ideas in a sentence. The conjunction *but* shows a contrast between two ideas. The conjunction *and* shows a similarity between two ideas.

Examples: I wanted to eat outside, **but** it was raining.
I like to travel, **but** no one else in my family does.

I wanted to eat outside, **and** my friends did, too.
I like to travel, **and** so do all of my friends.

Add the conjunction and *or* but *to each sentence.*

1. The captain expected to find someone on the *Marie Celeste*, _____ no one was there.

2. The last diary entry on the *Marie Celeste* was ten days old, _____ the food was only a few days old.

3. Nothing on the ship was missing, _____ the captain and crew were gone.

4. The Roanoke settlers didn't have enough food for the winter, _____ they lacked grain for their future crops.

5. Captain White was eager to see the settlers, _____ no one came to greet him.

6. People thought that the early Roanoke settlers had vanished forever, _____ there are people today who still have the same names.

7. The Easter Island statues are carved from stone, _____ some wear stone hats.

8. People in central Siberia saw a bright light, _____ seconds later they heard a tremendous explosion.

9. Trees were still black from the explosion, _____ many of them lay flat on the ground.

10. The Monarch butterflies make a very long trip south, _____ they always return to the same location.

b Spelling Review

1. Look at the words below, and then answer the questions.

Singular	Plural	Singular	Plural
toy	toys	navy	navies
holiday	holidays	story	stories
day	days	city	cities
donkey	donkeys	party	parties

   a. How do you form the plural of a noun that ends in a vowel plus -*y*?
   b. How do you form the plural of a noun that ends in a consonant plus -*y*?

2. Write the plural form of each noun.

   a. mystery _____
   b. donkey _____
   c. theory _____
   d. army _____
   e. tray _____
   f. enemy _____
   g. diary _____
   h. valley _____
   i. discovery _____
   j. worry _____

C Word Forms

Verb	Noun	Adjective
1. isolate	isolation	isolated
2. desert	desertion	deserted
3. inspect	inspection	inspected
4. mystify	mystery	mysterious
5. imagine	imagination	imaginative
6. explode	explosion	explosive
7. compare	comparison	comparable
8. suggest	suggestion	suggested
9. destroy	destruction	destructive

Put the correct word form in each blank. Use words from line 1 in item 1, and so on. Use the right verb forms and singular or plural nouns.

1. He lives in a very _____ area. I think his closest neighbor is 50 miles away.

2. When the ship started to sink, everyone _____ it.

3. There is going to be an important _____ tomorrow. I hope everything is ready when the boss comes to _____ the office.

4. We heard a _____ noise last night. However, the _____ was eventually explained. It was a white goat.

5. What an _____ that author has! In her last novel, she _____ she lived five hundred years ago in Hungary.

6. The gas _____ when it got hot. The _____ woke everyone up.

7. My brother _____ the two cars and decided to buy the smaller one.

8. Clare has a good _____. She thinks we should meet on Sunday.

9. It was a very _____ explosion. It _____ every house on our street.

d Regular and Irregular Verbs

Write the past tense of each verb. Then use the past tense in a sentence.

1. inspect _____
2. fight _____
3. vanish _____
4. settle _____
5. shake _____
6. come _____
7. find _____
8. hit _____
9. imagine _____
10. suggest _____

e Collocations

We often use certain adjectives and nouns together. For example, we say *a tall person* and *a high cliff*. We don't usually say *a high person* or *a tall cliff*.

Match the adjectives and nouns in the lists below. The first one is done for you.

Adjectives		**Nouns**
1. solemn	*d. face*	a. life
2. loud	_____	b. island
3. long	_____	c. cliff
4. noisy	_____	d. face
5. bright	_____	e. enemy
6. deserted	_____	f. classroom
7. hostile	_____	g. light
8. high	_____	h. explosion

f Writing

Choose one or more of these topics and write answers.

1. Which of the five mysteries was the strangest to you? Why?
2. Pretend that a member of the crew of the *Marie Celeste* wrote a message, put it in a bottle, and dropped the bottle in the ocean. You just found the bottle with the message. What does the message say?
3. Describe something mysterious—something you read or heard about.

a Before You Watch

You have read about Easter Island. For each of these sentences, write T *if the sentence is true. Write* F *if it is not true.*

_____ 1. Easter Island is one of the most isolated islands in the world.

_____ 2. The island is famous for its mysterious paintings.

_____ 3. Some of the statues on Easter Island are over 60 feet tall.

_____ 4. Easter Island is one of the largest islands in the world.

b As You Watch

There are some interesting facts in the video. As you watch, fill in the blanks in the sentences with some of the numbers from the list below.

| hundreds | 3,000 | 55 | 1914 | 111 |
| 20 | 60 | 1870s | thousands | 15,000 |

1. Some statues weigh _____ of tons.
2. They are as much as _____ meters, or _____ feet, high.
3. Tourism can have a downside for the island's _____ inhabitants.
4. By the _____, only _____ Easter Islanders remained.

C   After You Watch

Follow the directions to write on the map of Easter Island.

1. Draw an arrow pointing in the direction of South America.
2. Write *Pacific Ocean* and *Easter Island* on the appropriate lines on the map.
3. Moto Nui is an island off Easter Island's southwestern tip. Make a cross where it is on the map.
4. In one of the four circles on the map, write *N* for north.
5. Draw a triangle connecting the three main volcanoes of Ranu Kau, Maunga Terevaka, and Katiki.
6. The original inhabitants of Easter Island made the statues from huge stones lying near the volcanic crater at Rano Raraku. Then they pulled the statues to Vinapu, almost ten miles away. Draw a line from one place to the other.

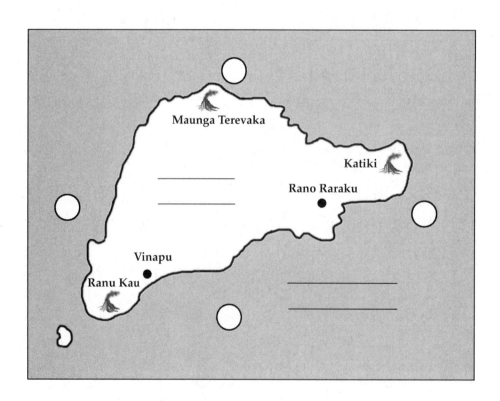

In the News

TEENAGERS VANISH IN WHIRLWIND

1. Look at the newspaper headline above; then use items from the squares below to make up your own headlines. Here are some verbs you might want to use:

discover   destroy   shake
damage   amaze   vanish
capture   throw   kick
disappear

teenagers   wrestler   scientists   customer   runners

explosion   whirlwind   tidal wave   meteor   sharks

2. *A baby-sitter was in charge of a small boy, Sammy. They were having a snack in the kitchen. She left the room to answer the phone. When she came back, she saw that Sammy had damaged many things. Work with a partner to find them. Below are some verbs you can use.*

damaged	opened	burned
broke	undid	wrote
removed	emptied	unrolled
tore	dropped	flooded

Example: Sammy tore the curtains. He cut the . . . .

Informal Usage

Often a word has two uses, one for formal speech and writing, and the other for everyday, or *informal*, speech. Your dictionary indicates whether a word has an informal meaning.

1. Read the dictionary entries below; then circle the number of the informal entry. The first one is done for you.

broke /broʊk/
1 *past tense of* break
②*adjective informal* without money: *I am broke.*

neat /nit/ *adjective*
1 in good order, *(synonym)* tidy: *His house is always neat and clean.*
2 skillfully done: *a neat way of saying something*
3 *informal* great, wonderful: *We had a neat time at the party.* —*adverb* **neatly;** —*noun* **neatness.**

lot /lɑt/ *noun*
1 a piece of land: *We own a small lot next to our house.*
2 *(no plural)* one's condition in life: *It was his lot to become a priest.*
3 *informal* **a lot** *(of)* or **lots** *(of)*: a large amount or number: *I like her a lot. He has lots of money, problems, etc.*

nut /nʌt/ *noun*
1 a fruit with a hard shell or its seed: *a candy made from fruit and nuts*
2 *informal* a person who seems very odd or crazy: *Stop acting like a nut!*
3 a small piece of metal with a hole in the middle, used with a bolt

kid /kɪd/ noun
1 *informal* a child
2 a young goat

noodle /'nudl/ *noun*
1 a long, narrow or wide, flat strip of pasta made from a mixture of flour, egg, and water: *Boil the noodles first.*
2 *informal* head: *You can figure it out; just use your noodle!*

? 159

2. *Decide whether the words in bold are used formally or informally. Put a check mark (✓) in the correct column:* Formal *or* Informal.

	Formal	Informal
a. I'm so **broke** I can't afford to buy lunch.	☐	☐
b. Fruit cake always contains raisins and **nuts.**	☐	☐
c. That was a really **neat** piece of music.	☐	☐
d. What's the name of your **kid** brother?	☐	☐
e. Julio's made a **lot** of enemies.	☐	☐
f. She always kept her room **neat** and tidy.	☐	☐

3. *Rewrite each sentence. Replace each boldfaced word with a synonym. The first one is done for you.*

a. My brother John is only a **kid.**
   My brother John is only a child.

b. He always acts like a **nut.**
   _____

c. That cake's got **lots** of cream in it.
   _____

e. Your sister's really **neat.**
   _____

f. I'm **broke,** but I have a credit card.
   _____

g. She's smart, but she doesn't use her **noodle.**
   _____

?

Business

© Peter Foley/EPA/Landov

Context Clues

Put a circle around the letter of the answer that means the same as the word in bold.

1. What a **contrast** there is between the two brothers! Charles is on the debating team. He's quiet and very studious. Jake is on the football team. He's talkative and very active in sports.
   a. argument
   b. great difference
   c. comparison
   d. question

2. They had a **misunderstanding.** He thought they agreed to meet at 5 o'clock. She thought they agreed to meet at 6 o'clock.
   a. lack of agreement about something
   b. relationship
   c. plan
   d. discovery

3. The hands on a clock **indicate** the time of day.
   a. prevent
   b. accept
   c. fill
   d. show

4. What is their **relationship?** Are they friends or business partners?
   a. work
   b. generation
   c. discovery
   d. connection

5. You can use **gestures** to communicate with someone who can't hear you.
   a. loud noises
   b. bright lights
   c. movements of the hands or head
   d. questions

6. Learning a foreign language is **challenging** for adults. It's much easier for children to learn another language.
   a. easy
   b. fun
   c. difficult
   d. clever

7. He doesn't want to drive me into the city, but he is **willing** to do it.
   a. nervous about
   b. against
   c. agreeing
   d. on time

8. Tell me some of the **customs** of your country. For example, are there any unusual ways of greeting people? What do you do on your important holidays?
   a. special thoughts
   b. special opinions
   c. special behaviors
   d. special answers

9. I have $9.50. That's **almost** ten dollars.
   a. exactly
   b. close to
   c. a lot more than
   d. a little more than

10. He's very good at **imitating** people. He can do politicians and movie actors, but he's best at **imitating** ordinary people.
    a. making friends with
    b. signing agreements with
    c. copying the actions of
    d. giving money to

11. Businesspeople often take their **clients** out to lunch. It's a good idea because they get to know each other better, and it makes the **clients** feel valued.
    a. customers
    b. friends
    c. wives
    d. offspring

12. What an **insult**! When I greeted her, she walked past me as if she didn't know me.
    a. stupid mistake
    b. happy answer
    c. unkind action or words
    d. funny word

Context Clues

lesson 1

The History of Money

© Mary Steinbacher/Photo Edit

Before You Read

1. How can you tell that the money in the picture is from different countries?

2. Why do coins come in different sizes?

3. Why do you think we have paper money?

164

1   The History of Money

coins

bills

Today, **currency** is a mixture of <u>coins</u> and paper money. But it wasn't always that way. Before people had **metal** coins and paper <u>bills</u>, they used a lot of unusual things for money. In one part of the world, for example, people used sharks' teeth for money. In some places, brightly colored feathers and rare seashells were money. People in one area even used the hair from elephants' tails for money.

No one knows for sure when people started using metal coins for money. The oldest coins are over 2,500 years old, so we know that people used coins a very long time ago. At first, people used <u>precious</u> metals, such as gold and silver, to make coins. They stamped the shape of a person or animal on each coin to <u>indicate</u> its value.

very valuable

show

In the 13th century, people in China used **iron** coins for their currency. These coins weren't **worth** very much, and people had to use many of them to buy things. Because it was <u>inconvenient</u> to carry so many of these coins, the government started making paper **receipts.** People took these receipts to banks and **traded** them for coins. This was the first example of paper money.

not easy

Today, most countries use a mixture of coins and paper bills for their currency. In the United States, the paper bills are all the same size and color. For example, the $1 bill is the same size and color as the $100 bill. In many other countries, the bills have different sizes and colors. The smaller bills are worth less money. This makes it easier for people to tell the value of their money.

In 2002, twelve European countries started using a completely new currency. It's called the *euro*. Many Europeans miss their old currencies, but now it's easier to move money from one country to another.

Here are a few more **fascinating** facts about the   very interesting
history of money.

- Feathers were the lightest money ever used. People on the Pacific island of Santa Cruz used them.
- Stones were the heaviest money ever used. People on the Pacific island of Yap used them. Some weighed over 500 pounds!
- The smallest money ever used was in Greece. The coins were made of metal, but they were smaller than an apple seed.

a Vocabulary

Put the right word in each blank. The sentences are from the text.

currency	worth	facts	precious	coins
iron	bills	metal	inconvenient	
receipts	indicate	fascinating	traded	

1. Because it was _____ to carry so many coins, the government started making paper _____.

2. At first, people used _____ metals, such as gold and silver, to make coins.

3. Here are a few more _____ _____ about the history of money.

4. People took these receipts to banks and _____ them for coins.

5. Today, _____ is a mixture of _____ and paper money.

6. These coins weren't _____ very much, and people had to use many of them to buy things.

7. Before people had _____ coins and paper _____, they used a lot of unusual things for money.

8. They stamped the shape of a person or animal on each coin to _____ its value.

9. In the 13th century, people in China used _____ coins for their currency.

166

b Vocabulary: New Context

Put the right word in each blank.

facts	precious	coins	worth	bill
indicates	iron	metal	inconvenient	
receipt	traded	fascinating	currency	

1. Each country has its own _____. In Mexico, it's the peso, and in Japan, it's the yen.

2. A newspaper reporter needs all the _____ to write a good story.

3. My friends are more _____ to me than the most valuable jewels.

4. She spends most of her free time taking photographs. It's a _____ hobby.

5. When you buy something in a store, they usually put the _____ in the bag.

6. _____ is a common kind of metal. It has been used in _____.

7. Can you change a twenty-dollar _____ for me?

8. When people smile, it usually _____ that they are happy.

9. The bus is cheap, but it's a little _____. It makes ten stops before it gets to the city.

10. Which car is _____ more money?

11. Paul _____ his soccer ball for his friend's basketball. I think they're both happy.

12. _____ is stronger than paper.

c | Vocabulary Review

Put the right word in each blank.

tiny	war	prevent	sink
odd	destroyed	flat	suggest
volunteers	identical	realize	

1. Can you _____ a good restaurant around here?
2. The hole in my shirt is _____. I don't think anyone will see it.
3. I can't put the table here, because the ground isn't _____.
4. She looked so healthy that I didn't _____ that she was sick.
5. There is an _____ smell in the room. I can't identify it.
6. If you throw a stone in the water, it will _____.
7. My brothers bought _____ cars, but they didn't do it on purpose.
8. There was a _____ in the United States in the 1860s. Many people died.
9. Chris was lucky he didn't get hurt. His car was _____.
10. That high fence helps to _____ people from entering.
11. I need some _____ to help me organize the party.

d | Comprehension: Multiple Choice

Put a circle around the letter of the best answer.

1. In China in the 13th century, coins were made from _____.
   a. gold
   b. copper
   c. silver
   d. iron
2. The oldest coins are about _____ years old.
   a. 6,000
   b. 8,000
   c. 2,500
   d. 800
3. In most countries, the _____ is a mixture of paper and coins.
   a. dollar
   b. currency
   c. precious metal
   d. receipt

4. People in China traded paper money for coins at _____.
   a. banks   c. warehouses
   b. teahouses   d. government offices

5. Paper became a form of money because _____.
   a. it was cheap
   b. it was easy to carry
   c. it was heavier than metal
   d. the government didn't have any metal

6. The Chinese started to use _____ instead of carrying around heavy
   iron coins.
   a. sharks' teeth   c. receipts
   b. gold and silver   d. dollars

7. _____ were the lightest money ever.
   a. sharks' teeth   c. seashells
   b. feathers   d. stones

8. _____ were the heaviest money ever used.
   a. sharks' teeth   c. seashells
   b. feathers   d. stones

9. Some of the stone money weighed over _____ pounds.
   a. 500   c. 600
   b. 60   d. 5,000

10. The smallest money ever was used in _____.
    a. Greece   c. Italy
    b. China   d. the Pacific islands

11. The smallest coins ever were about the size of _____.
    a. postage stamps   c. apple seeds
    b. apple cores   d. seashells

12. The bills of many countries have _____ sizes and colors.
    a. the same   c. inconvenient
    b. different   d. identical

Questions

The asterisk (*) means you have to think of the answer. You cannot find it in the text.

1. What are some of the things people used before they had coins and bills?
*2. How did people choose the things they used for money?
3. Do we know for certain when people first used metal coins?
4. What is the date of the earliest coins?
5. What metal did people first use to make coins?
*6. How do most countries indicate the value of coins today?
7. What metal did Chinese people use for coins in the 13th century?
8. What country made the first paper money?
9. Why did they make paper money?
10. Are all paper bills in the United States the same size and color?
11. Are bills the same size and color in other countries?
12. What is the euro?

 Main Idea

Which is the main idea of this lesson? Choose one.

1. In the early days, many unusual things were used for money.
2. Paper currency started in China in the 13th century.
3. Coins and paper eventually replaced the early types of money.

170

lesson 2

Mass Marketing

© Lester Lefkowitz/CORBIS

Before You Read

1. A logo is a symbol chosen by a business to use on its
   products, advertisements, and so on. What logos do you see
   in the picture?

2. Are you familiar with any of these companies?

3. How do companies get people to buy their products?

171

Lesson 2: Mass Marketing

2   Mass Marketing

In the 1880s, people drank John Pemberton's tonic to **cure** headaches. It wasn't a very popular drink, and he sold only about a dozen drinks a day. That's why Pemberton was **willing** to sell the rights to his medicinal drink. The buyer, Asa Griggs Candler, paid just $2,300 for the rights to Coca-Cola. Today, Coca-Cola (or Coke) is worth billions of dollars. It **controls** 50 percent of the world **market** in soft drinks.

make better

How did Coca-Cola become so popular? One answer is that Asa Candler was a very **clever** businessperson. He was one of the first people to use **mass** **marketing.** How did he do this? First, he made his product **unique.** When he bought the rights to Coca-Cola, it came in ordinary bottles. It looked like every other drink on the market. To make Coca-Cola look different, Candler modernized the bottles. He also made an eye-catching **logo** for his product. When other companies tried to **imitate** Coca-Cola's name, Candler took them to **court.**

smart

selling a product in large numbers

different from all others, special

copy

In addition to the unique bottle and logo, Candler spent a lot of time and money **advertising** his product. He used advertising to make a powerful **image** of Coca-Cola in the minds of his customers. He gave away free bottles of Coke. He put the name of his drink on pencils, trays, Japanese fans, matches, and many other things. Then he gave the things to people for free. He advertised Coca-Cola in the newspaper and painted the words "Drink Coca-Cola" on the sides of buildings and barns. By 1902, Coca-Cola was the best known product in the United States.

picture

Candler was also able to make **memorable** advertisements. They often had catchy slogans such as "The Pause That Refreshes." He also used famous athletes to advertise his product. They helped people to think of Coca-Cola as a delicious drink for everyone.

easy to remember

Today, businesses all over the world use mass marketing, but the makers of Coke were the first.

172

a Vocabulary

Put the right word in each blank. The sentences are from the text.

controls	willing	clever	logo
unique	mass marketing	court	memorable
advertising	imitate	image	cure
market			

1. One answer is that Asa Candler was a very _____ businessperson.
2. He also made an eye-catching _____ for his product.
3. That's why Pemberton was _____ to sell the rights to his medicinal drink.
4. First, he made his product _____.
5. In the 1880s, people drank John Pemberton's tonic to _____ headaches.
6. In addition to the unique bottle and logo, Candler spent a lot of time and money _____ his product.
7. It _____ 50 percent of the world _____ in soft drinks.
8. He used advertising to make a powerful _____ of Coca-Cola in the minds of his customers.
9. He was one of the first people to use _____.
10. Candler was also able to make _____ advertisements.
11. When other companies tried to _____ Coca-Cola's name, Candler took them to _____.

b Vocabulary: New Context

Put the right word in each blank.

clever	control	willing	market
unique	mass-marketing	court	memorable
image	advertise	imitate	cure
logos			

1. Our trip was not very _____. Nothing interesting happened.

2. Egypt is _____. It's the only country with such famous pyramids.

3. I am _____ to drive you to the city, but I can't do it today.

4. Large businesses pay millions to have artists make up _____ for their products.

5. He lost _____ of the car when it hit the wall.

6. Do you think we will ever have a _____ for cancer?

7. There isn't a large _____ for fax machines anymore. Most people use the Internet instead.

8. That fast-food company used _____ methods to get ahead of all its competition.

9. I know they _____ their product in the newspaper. I saw it there last week.

10. I have an _____ of him as a very unfriendly person, but his employees say he is really warm and fun-loving.

11. My boss is very _____. She can fix anything.

12. A few kinds of birds can _____ the sounds of other animals. A parrot, for example, can make the sound of a cat or even say a few words.

13. Our neighbors are fighting over the land between their houses. They will probably take their fight to _____.

c Vocabulary Review

Match the word in Column A with the word in Column B that means the same. The first one is done for you.

Column A

1. indicate   *l. show*
2. site
3. explode
4. odd
5. precious
6. fascinate
7. vanish
8. hostile
9. absent
10. identical
11. rapidly
12. bitter

Column B

a. disappear
b. blow up
c. valuable
d. not present
e. quickly
f. not sweet
g. same
h. location
i. strange
j. unfriendly
k. interest
l. show

d Comprehension: Multiple Choice

Put a circle around the letter of the best answer.

1. Coca-Cola controls _____ of the world market in soft drinks.
   a. all   b. 80 percent   c. half   d. more than 50 percent

2. At first, people drank Coca-Cola as a _____ drink.
   a. mass-marketed   b. chocolate   c. medicinal   d. breakfast

3. Coca-Cola has _____ of the world soft-drink market.
   a. 80 percent   b. 30 percent   c. 50 percent   d. almost 100 percent

4. Asa Candler _____ the original Coca-Cola bottles.
   a. changed   b. liked   c. mass marketed   d. used

5. Among other places, Candler advertised his products on _____.
   a. airplanes   b. customers   c. wall   d. buses

6. By 1902, Coca-Cola was the _____ product in the United States.
   a. cheapest   b. best-known   c. most expensive   d. healthiest

7. The makers of Coke used _____ to sell their product.
   a. mass marketing   b. advertising   c. famous people   d. a, b, and c

175

8. Candler used an eye-catching logo for his product. "Eye-catching" refers to something _____.
   a. you can't see
   b. delicious
   c. you can't avoid looking at
   d. you don't want to look at

9. Candler gave away _____ to promote Coca-Cola.
   a. the unique logo
   b. time and money
   c. the rights to the drink
   d. many small things

10. Coke used slogans to advertise its product. Slogans are _____.
    a. popular music
    b. memorable phrases
    c. free things
    d. simple images

11. Candler chose _____ to be in his advertisements.
    a. athletes
    b. movie stars
    c. children
    d. well-known writers

12. Candler bought the rights to Coca-Cola from _____.
    a. the inventor of a medicinal tonic
    b. a well-known businessman
    c. a doctor
    d. a carpenter

e Questions

The asterisk (*) means you have to think of the answer. You cannot find it in the text.

1. Who was the inventor of Coca-Cola?
2. In the beginning, what was it sold as?
3. Why was Pemberton willing to sell the rights to his tonic?
4. What did Candler use to make his drink popular?
*5. Can you think of other products that are sold through mass marketing?
6. Can you name the two changes that Candler made to give his product a new look?
7. What happened when other companies tried to imitate Coca-Cola?
8. How did Candler advertise Coca-Cola?
9. Why did Candler give people free bottles of Coca-Cola?
*10. Can you think of a memorable slogan?

f Main Idea

Which is the main idea of this lesson? Choose one.

1. Mass marketing changed Coca-Cola from a small company into a worldwide business.
2. People in almost every country in the world drink Coca-Cola.
3. Logos and catchy slogans are common ways to market a product.

Unit 5: Business

Inflation

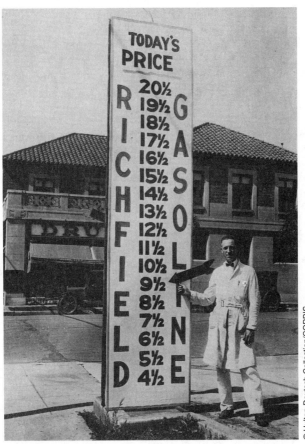

© Hulton-Deutsch Collection/CORBIS

Before You Read

1. How can you tell that the picture is an old photograph?

2. What is the reason for so many different numbers?

3. What is the arrow for?

3   Inflation

Workers usually get paid once a week, but in Germany in the early 1920s they got paid twice a day. Besides that, they had an extra half-hour every morning to go shopping for food. If that sounds wonderful, let's see what one normal day in 1923 was really like.

At 11:30 A.M., work stopped at the **factory,** and Karl Hoffman <u>lined up</u> with the other workers. The **boss** gave him two huge bags. "Here's your morning's salary," the boss said. "Fifty million German marks in **cash**." Karl **loaded** his salary into a wheelbarrow and ran in the **direction** of a big produce store. Inside, he stood in a long line of people, all with huge bags of money. "How much are the onions?" he asked the sales clerk. "Twenty-five million marks for one," she answered. Karl bought two onions and gave her the **contents** of his wheelbarrow. Then he returned to work for the afternoon.

When Karl arrived home in the evening, he gave his wife the two onions. "I worked all morning to buy two onions," he told her. "I passed the produce store on my way home, and in just a few hours, food doubled in price. Onions now cost 50 million marks each. My afternoon's salary is **almost** worthless. It will buy only one onion. I'm going to burn the bills for heat." He threw the paper money into the fire.

This story was typical for millions of Germans in the early 1920s. People burned money for heat. They worked for 3 days to buy a pound of butter, and 20 weeks to buy a suit. In the chart below, you can see how the value of the German mark <u>dropped</u> in just 9 years. In 1914, about 4 marks equaled a dollar. Nine years later, about 4 trillion marks equaled a dollar.

Glossary:
formed a line
person in charge at work

bills and coins

anything that is inside of something else

went down, decreased

Inflation in Germany from 1914 to 1923

The column on the right shows how many German marks were paid for one U.S. dollar. For example, in July 1923, one U.S. dollar was worth 353,412 German marks.

July 1914	4.2 marks = $1
January 1919	8.9 marks = $1
July 1919	14.0 marks = $1
January 1920	64.8 marks = $1
January 1922	191.8 marks = $1
July 1922	493.2 marks = $1
January 1923	17,972.0 marks = $1
July 1923	353,412.0 marks = $1
August 1923	4,620,455.0 marks = $1
September 1923	98,860,000.0 marks = $1
October 1923	25,260,208,000.0 marks = $1
November 1923	4,200,000,000,000.0 marks = $1

What took place during those 9 years is called runaway **inflation.** Prices increased by millions of marks in a few hours. It's normal for countries to have a little inflation, but usually it's very slow. Prices increase by a few cents every year. For example, in 1926, a U.S. postage stamp cost just 2 cents. Today, it costs almost 40 cents. In **contrast** to that example of normal inflation, the German government printed the postage stamp again and again in the early 1920s. Eventually, a postage stamp cost over a million marks. And what happened to Karl? He **survived.** The government changed the name of the currency. It printed new money, and prices went down.

a Vocabulary

Put the right word in each blank. The sentences are from the text.

contrast	cash	inflation	survived	factory	loaded
almost	contents	lined up	dropped	boss	direction

1. The _____ gave him two huge bags.
2. At 11:30 A.M., work stopped at the _____, and Karl Hoffman _____ with the other workers.
3. In the chart below, you can see how the value of the German mark _____ in just 9 years.
4. What took place during those 9 years is called runaway _____.
5. In _____ to that example of normal inflation, the German government printed the postage stamp again and again in the early 1920s.
6. My afternoon's salary is _____ worthless.
7. And what happened to Karl? He _____.
8. Karl bought two onions and gave her the _____ of his wheelbarrow.
9. Fifty million German marks in _____.
10. Karl _____ his salary into a wheelbarrow and ran in the _____ of a big produce store.

b Vocabulary: New Context

Put the right word in each blank.

inflation	contents	drop	survive	contrast	boss
almost	direction	line up	factory	load	cash

1. Please don't _____ the statue. It might break.
2. Tony had a serious operation; however, the doctors say he will _____.
3. She _____ fell off the boat. Luckily, her sister prevented her from falling.
4. When the price of goods rises suddenly, it's called _____.
5. I think the bank is north of here. I hope I'm going in the right _____.
6. I work in a _____ that makes cars.

180

7. Can you help me _____ these stones into the truck? They're very heavy.

8. The pale gray walls _____ nicely with the reds and purples of the carpet on the floor.

9. She took the _____ out of the bag and used the bag for shopping.

10. I'm going to the bank to get $100 in _____.

11. Could you please _____ in alphabetical order?

12. I want to ask my _____ to increase my salary.

C Vocabulary Review

Put the right word in each blank.

cure	fact	worth	control
inconvenient	tag	shortage	willing
survive	delicious	amount	fascinating

1. I can work on Saturday, but I'm not _____ to work on Sunday.

2. You can't _____ in very cold water for very long.

3. It's important to _____ your temper and the car when you are driving.

4. I can't stop reading this book. It's _____.

5. There is no _____ for his disease, but it won't shorten his life.

6. In a store, each thing usually has a price _____. It tells you how much the thing costs.

7. Gold is _____ more than silver.

8. There is a _____ of water now because it didn't rain much during the spring.

9. If it's not _____ for you, can you give me a ride to work?

10. Your statement is an opinion. It's not a _____.

11. I don't like cooked carrots, but I think raw carrots are _____.

12. Do you know the exact _____ of gasoline in the car?

181

d Comprehension: Sequence

Number these sentences in the right order. The first one is done for you.

_____ He stopped when he got to the produce store.

_____ The boss gave Karl two huge bags of money for his morning's salary.

_____ There was a long line of people inside the produce store.

_____ Karl bought two onions.

_____ Karl Hoffman lined up with the other workers.

_____ He threw his afternoon's salary into the fire.

_____ He went back to work for the afternoon.

___1___ Work stopped at the factory at 11:30 A.M.

_____ He went home for the evening.

_____ Karl loaded his salary into a wheelbarrow and started running.

e Questions

The asterisk (*) means you have to think of the answer. You cannot find it in the text.

1. What was unusual about a worker's salary in Germany in the early 1920s?
*2. In 1923, why did workers get extra time to go food shopping?
*3. In 1923, why did workers get paid twice a day?
4. What did Karl Hoffman do with his morning's salary?
5. What did he do with his afternoon's salary? Why?
6. What happened to the price of food in that one day?
7. Look at the chart on page 179. How much was a German mark worth compared to the U.S. dollar in July 1914? How much was a German mark worth in November 1923?
8. How much did a postage stamp cost in the United States in 1926? How much does it cost today?
9. How is runaway inflation different from normal inflation?
*10. What country has high inflation now? What is its rate of inflation?

f Main Idea

Which is the main idea of this lesson? Choose one.

1. In November 1923, a U.S. dollar was worth over a trillion German marks.
2. Inflation was so bad in Germany in the early 1920s that workers got paid twice a day.
3. A little inflation is normal, but runaway inflation can cause serious problems.

lesson

4

Doing Business
Around the World

© Charles Gupton/Stone/getty images

Before You Read

1. The people in the picture are bowing. In what other ways do people greet each other?

2. What do you need to know to do business in another country?

4 Doing Business Around the World

People from different **cultures** have different ways of doing things. For example, in some parts of the world, people read the date 2/1/2005 as the second of January in 2005. They put the day before the month. In other parts of the world, people read this date as February 1, 2005. They put the month before the day.

A simple **gesture** can also have a different meaning from one culture to another. The thumbs-up sign means "excellent" in the United States, but it's an <u>insult</u> in parts of Africa. Moving the head up and down means "yes" in Europe and the United States. However, in Greece and Turkey, it means "no." To point a finger at someone is okay in Canada, but it's <u>rude</u> in Japan.

For businesspeople, differences like this can cause serious **misunderstandings.** These misunderstandings can destroy business **relationships.** To avoid this, many businesspeople attend classes to learn about other cultures. They study the <u>customs</u> of other countries. Here are a few things they learn.

Greeting <u>clients</u> correctly is important in the business world. However, customs for greeting people vary from one culture to another. North American men and women often shake hands when they meet. In Japan, people often bow. People from Thailand put their hands together as if praying and then bow the head. In some Arab countries, men don't shake hands with women from outside the family.

Entertaining is important in the business world. It's often necessary to invite a client to lunch or dinner. However, customs about eating also vary from culture to culture. Some people don't eat meat; others don't drink alcohol. In the West, people eat with knives and forks; in the East, they eat with chopsticks. In some

an unkind action or words

not polite

ways of behaving

customers

 185

cultures, it's okay to **discuss** business while eating.   talk about
In other cultures, talking about business during a
meal is rude. Businesspeople need to know about
these differences.

Sometimes businesspeople visit the homes of their
clients. In most countries, it's the custom to take a small
gift. But what do you take? Again, the customs vary. For
example, in England, giving a knife is bad luck. In some
countries, it's rude to give white flowers or a watch or
clock. Another difficulty is how much money to spend
on a gift. If you spend only a little money, you might
appear **stingy.** If you spend too much, the gift might   not wanting to spend
look like a **bribe.** In Malaysia and many other countries,   money or give away
there are **laws** against bribery.   anything

Doing business with people from different cultures is
both fascinating and **challenging.** Many businesspeople
try to learn about other cultures. They do their best to
avoid cultural misunderstandings.

a   Vocabulary

Put the right word in each blank. The sentences are from the text.

bribe	customs	gesture	relationships
challenging	cultures	insult	misunderstandings
clients	discuss	laws	stingy
rude			

1. To point a finger at someone is okay in Canada, but it's
   _____ in Japan.

2. Greeting _____ correctly is important in the
   business world.

3. These misunderstandings can destroy business _____.

4. Doing business with people from different cultures is both fascinating and _____.

5. In some cultures, it's okay to _____ business while eating.

6. People from different _____ have different ways of doing things.

7. For businesspeople, differences like this can cause serious _____.

8. If you spend too much, the gift might look like a _____.

9. In Malaysia and many other countries, there are _____ against bribery.

10. The thumbs-up sign means "excellent" in the United States, but it's an _____ in parts of Africa.

11. They study the _____ of other countries.

12. A simple _____ can also have a different meaning from one culture to another.

13. If you spend only a little money, you might appear _____.

b Vocabulary: New Context

Put the right word in each blank.

cultures	rude	gesturing	relationship
challenging	custom	insulted	stingy
discussed	law	client	misunderstanding
bribe			

1. In some parts of the world, it is against the _____ to drive and talk on a cell phone.

2. Running a mile is more _____ than walking a mile.

3. If businesspeople want to have a good _____ with a _____, they need to talk to the person frequently.

4. I was angry with my brother, but then I realized he didn't do anything wrong. We just had a _____.

5. There is a big cake on the table. A _____ person would give his friend only a tiny piece.

6. We _____ the problem for several hours, but we still couldn't agree.

7. He _____ me when he left without saying goodbye.

8. The policeman is _____ at you to stop. You should stop now.

9. Parents sometimes try to _____ their children. They give them candy to make them quiet.

10. I think it's _____ to read someone else's mail. What do you think?

11. Traveling helps you learn about other _____.

12. Iran has a very interesting _____. On the last day of its New Year's celebration, the men jump over a fire.

c Vocabulary Review

Match the word in Column A with the word or phrase in Column B that means the same. The first one is done for you.

Column A

1. inflation   *j. price increase*
2. drop   _____
3. fascinating   _____
4. solemn   _____
5. inspect   _____
6. contrast   _____
7. frequently   _____
8. cash   _____
9. survive   _____
10. retire   _____
11. bury   _____
12. wealthy   _____
13. almost   _____
14. rare   _____

Column B

a. serious
b. look at carefully
c. paper money and coins
d. nearly
e. unusual
f. stop working
g. difference
h. rich
i. go down
j. price increase
k. interesting
l. often
m. continue to live
n. put in the ground

d Comprehension: Multiple Choice

Put a circle around the letter of the best answer.

1. The thumbs-up sign is an example of a _____.
   a. gesture   c. client
   b. law   d. relationship

2. Businesspeople learn about the customs of other cultures because they don't want to _____ their foreign clients.
   a. insult   c. help
   b. bribe   d. do business with

3. Cultures are _____ in different parts of the world.
   a. similar   c. different
   b. identical   d. rude

4. Pointing at someone is _____ in Canada.
   a. clever
   c. crazy
   b. bribery
   d. okay

5. One way people greet each other is by _____.
   a. discussing
   c. entertaining
   b. bowing
   d. insulting

6. In England, some people say that giving a knife is _____.
   a. bad luck
   c. good luck
   b. a bribe
   d. rude

7. If you do business in Japan, you probably shouldn't _____.
   a. give a gift
   c. point
   b. bow
   d. use chopsticks

8. It's challenging to do business with foreigners because _____.
   a. there is a lot to learn
   b. you can't make simple gestures
   c. entertaining is fun
   d. they are friendly

9. A client might think that a very expensive gift is a _____.
   a. law
   c. bribe
   b. greeting
   d. misunderstanding

10. There are laws against bribery _____.
    a. only in Malaysia
    c. in many countries
    b. everywhere
    d. in a few countries

e Questions

The asterisk (*) means you have to think of the answer. You cannot find it in the text.

*1. How does a South American write this date in numbers: the thirteenth of July in 1948?

*2. How does a North American write this date in numbers: the twentieth of December in 1948?

*3. How do you write this date using only numbers: the thirtieth of April in 2003?

4. How do people indicate "yes" in the United States? How do people indicate "no" in Turkey?

*5. How do you indicate "yes" in your country?

6. What do businesspeople in North America usually do when they meet?

7. What are some different ways that people greet each other?

*8. Why is entertaining important in the business world?
 9. What do businesspeople in Japan do when they meet?
*10. How can misunderstandings destroy business relationships?
*11. What do people eat with in China?
*12. Why do you think giving a knife as a gift in England is bad luck?

 ## Main Idea

Which is the main idea of this lesson? Choose one.

1. It can be difficult to do business in foreign countries.
2. It's a good idea to learn the customs of a place before doing business there.
3. Serious misunderstandings can destroy business relationships.

Lesson 4: Doing Business Around the World

lesson

5

Plastic Money

© David Young-Wolff/Photo Edit

Before You Read

1. How often do you use a credit card?

2. Do you think it's important to have a credit card? Why or why not?

3. Do you think young people should have credit cards? Why or why not?

5   Plastic Money

How do you pay for things? Do you usually use cash, or do you like to pay by **credit** card? If you are like a lot of people, you probably have at least one credit card in your wallet. Also, you might use it more often than you probably should.

Credit cards first became popular in the 1920s. Back then, individual businesses, such as hotels and oil companies, gave credit cards to their best customers. Unlike today's credit cards, customers could use these cards only at the store or business that gave out the card. Customers also had to pay their bill **in full.** They couldn't pay for something a little at a time.

completely

The first **multipurpose** credit card was the idea of a businessman named Frank McNamara. He got the idea one evening when he took some business clients to dinner. At the end of the meal, McNamara discovered that he couldn't pay the bill. He didn't have any cash with him! Luckily, his wife had some cash with her, and she paid the bill. After that experience, McNamara decided to find a way to allow people without cash to pay for meals in restaurants.

having more than one
use or purpose

In 1950, McNamara started a credit card company called Diners Club. Unlike earlier credit cards, this card could be used by customers at a variety of restaurants. When a customer paid for a meal by credit card, Diners Club paid the restaurant. At the end of the month, Diners Club sent a bill to the customer and collected the money. Customers liked the card because they didn't have to carry around a lot of cash. Restaurant **owners** quickly learned to like the card, too. Why? They discovered that customers usually spent more money when they could pay by credit card.

In its first year of business, Diners Club **issued** credit cards to 200 customers. These customers could use the Diners Club card at 27 different restaurants in New

gave out

York. Today, Diners Club has about 8 million customers, and they can use their cards in over 7.6 million businesses in more than 200 countries.

Soon after the appearance of Diners Club, banks decided to get **involved** in the credit card business. In 1956, Bank of America **offered** a new kind of credit card. With this card, you could either pay your bill in full at the end of the month or make smaller monthly payments. If you didn't pay in full, however, you had to pay **interest** on your **debt.**

Credit cards started as a convenience for customers. Businesses used them to hold on to their most valued customers. Credit cards are still a convenience, but they are also very **profitable** for banks and other issuers.

a Vocabulary

Put the right word in each blank. The sentences are from the text.

issued	debt	involved	profitable
interest	in full	offered	owners
multipurpose	credit		

1. Soon after the appearance of Diners Club, banks decided to get
   _____ in the credit card business.

2. If you didn't pay in full, however, you had to pay
   _____ on your _____.

3. Restaurant _____ quickly learned to like the card, too.

4. Credit cards are still a convenience, but they are also very
   _____ for banks and other issuers.

5. In 1956, Bank of America _____ a new kind of credit card.
6. Do you usually use cash, or do you like to pay by _____ card?
7. In its first year of business, Diners Club _____ credit cards to 200 customers.
8. Customers also had to pay their bill _____.
9. The first _____ credit card was the idea of a businessman named Frank McNamara.

b Vocabulary: New Context

Put the right word in each blank.

involved	issues	interest	own
in full	credit	debt	profit
multipurpose	offered		

1. He bought his house for $100,000 and sold it for $125,000. He made a _____ of $25,000.
2. Do you _____ your car or does the bank?
3. If you put your money into a savings account at a bank, the bank pays you _____ every month.
4. She doesn't want to be in _____, so she always pays her monthly bills _____.
5. I _____ him $1,000 for the old car, but he refused to sell it to me.
6. If you pay your bills on time, you will have good _____.
7. I bought some _____ paper to use with both my copy machine and my printer.
8. Every year, the post office _____ beautiful new stamps.
9. I don't want to get _____ in her problems.

c Vocabulary Review

Underline the word that does not belong in each group.

1. coin, bills, clients, credit cards
2. amount, boss, client, customer
3. dessert, snack, meal, medal
4. rude, stingy, clever, iron
5. discuss, disappear, explain, report
6. factory, job site, island, office
7. insult, criticize, curse, prevent
8. fascinating, inconvenient, clever, interesting

d Comprehension: True/False/No Information

Write T if the sentence is true. Write F if it is false. Write NI if no information about the sentence was given in the text.

_____ 1. Credit cards were popular in the 1800s.

_____ 2. The first credit cards were multipurpose.

_____ 3. Shoe stores were among the first businesses to give credit cards to their best customers.

_____ 4. When you pay in full, you pay the whole amount.

_____ 5. Frank McNamara was a businessman.

_____ 6. McNamara's wife always paid for her husband's meals at restaurants.

_____ 7. McNamara started the Diners Club credit card.

_____ 8. Diners Club was a store that sold things.

_____ 9. Diners Club started as a small business, but now it's a big business.

_____10. Banks make money on credit cards by charging interest.

 Questions

The asterisk (*) means you have to think of the answer. You cannot find it in the text.

1. Why did businesses give out credit cards in the 1920s?
2. What was different about the Diners Club credit card?
3. Why did Frank McNamara start a credit card company?
4. Why did customers like the Diners Club card?
5. Why did restaurant owners like the card?
6. How many customers did Diners Club have in its first year?
*7. Why did banks want to start issuing credit cards?
8. What was different about bank credit cards?
*9. What does it mean to be in debt?
*10. Why are credit cards a profitable business for banks?

 Main Idea

Which is the main idea of this lesson? Choose one.

1. Credit cards are a profitable business for banks.
2. Credit cards are dangerous for people who like to shop.
3. Today's credit cards are different from the first credit cards.

Word Study

a   Gerunds

A *gerund* is the *-ing* form of a verb. The boldfaced words in the examples below are gerunds.

Examples: Our cat Michy spends a lot of time **sleeping.**
When she is not asleep, she enjoys **looking** out the window.

We often use a gerund after these verbs and expressions:

enjoy	don't mind	dislike
remember	finish	stop
spend time	spend money	start

Write the gerund form of each verb.

Verb	Gerund	Verb	Gerund
imitate	_____	sell	_____
market	_____	watch	_____
read	_____	use	_____
discuss	_____	talk	_____
insult	_____	spend	_____

Choose a gerund from the list above to complete each sentence.

1. Pemberton didn't mind _____ the rights to his medicinal tonic, because it wasn't very popular.

2. Candler spent a lot of time _____ Coca-Cola.

3. A lot of people enjoy _____ politics.

4. I don't mind _____ money on something that is well made.

5. Do you remember _____ that book about inflation?

6. A lot of people, myself included, dislike _____ ads on television.

7. Do you know when people started _____ coins for money?

8. Soft drink companies stopped _____ Coca-Cola when Candler took them to court.

9. That shopkeeper enjoys _____ his customers. Soon he won't have any left.

10. I don't remember _____ to him on the telephone.

b Adjectives with -ive

Add the suffix -ive to each verb to form an adjective. Write the adjectives in the blanks.

Verb	Adjective
object	_____
invent	_____
reflect	_____
suggest	_____
express	_____

Drop the final -e on these verbs and then add -ive. Write the adjectives in the blanks.

Verb	Adjective
imitate	_____
indicate	_____

Drop the final -e on these verbs and then add -ative. Write the adjectives in the blanks.

Verb	Adjective
imagine	_____
compare	_____

C Word Forms

Verb	Noun	Adjective
1. discuss	discussion	discussed
2. imitate	imitation	imitative
3. advertise	advertisement	advertised
4. challenge	challenge	challenging
5. compare	comparison	comparative
6. direct	direction	(none)
7. fascinate	fascination	fascinating
8. imagine	imagination	imaginative
9. survive	survival	surviving
10. discover	discovery	discovered

Put the correct word form in each blank. Use words from line 1 in item 1, and so on. Use the right verb forms and singular and plural nouns.

1. We _____ the marketing program for several hours. When the _____ finally ended, everyone was in a hurry to leave.

2. Her _____ of Shirley is very good. I wish I could _____ people as well as she does.

3. Our company _____ its product on radio and television. These _____ cost a lot of money.

4. He _____ everyone to a singing contest. None of us can sing very well, so his competition was not very _____.

5. He's making a _____ study of two types of cars. He's going to _____ their cost and their reliability.

6. I gave her _____ to my house, but she lost them. Luckily, a policeman was able to _____ her here.

7. She has a _____ for family history. She is especially _____ by her mother's family.

8. Advertising people have great _____. Their
   advertisements are very _____.
9. Their _____ depended on collecting enough
   food for winter. They can't _____
   without food.
10. In what year did scientists _____ the cause of
    the explosion? Did any newspapers report their
    _____?

d Past Tense Review

Write the past tense of each verb.

1. offer   _____
2. issue   _____
3. misunderstand _____
4. insult   _____
5. find out   _____
6. run   _____
7. discover   _____
8. prevent   _____
9. bribe   _____
10. explode   _____
11. worry   _____
12. discuss   _____

e   Collocations

We often use certain verbs and nouns together. For example, we say *pay interest* and *get interest*. We don't usually say *need interest* or *cause interest*.

Choose a noun to complete each sentence below. (More than one answer may be possible.) Then ask a classmate your questions.

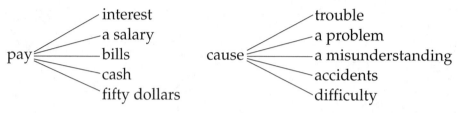

pay
- interest
- a salary
- bills
- cash
- fifty dollars

cause
- trouble
- a problem
- a misunderstanding
- accidents
- difficulty

1. Do you usually pay _____ when you buy food?
2. Do you usually pay your _____ on time?
3. Would you pay _____ for a movie ticket?
4. What causes you _____ when you are learning a new language?
5. What causes the most _____ on the road?
6. Did you ever cause _____ in school? What did you do?

f   Writing

Choose one or more of these topics and write answers.

1. In your opinion, was Asa Candler a good businessperson? Why or why not?
2. What are three things a foreign businessperson should know about your culture?
3. Imagine that the experts are predicting runaway inflation in the near future. What are you going to do to prepare for it? Describe your actions.

a Before You Watch

These words will help you understand the video. Read the words and their definitions.

estimate: to make a guess about an amount
script: writing
double digits: numbers from 10 to 99
sponsor: a group or business that helps pay for something

Now, choose one of the words above for each of the sentences below. You will hear similar sentences in the video.

1. The familiar red-and-white _____ can be seen in subway stations and street corners all over the world.
2. Sales will jump by _____ in Europe.
3. Coca-Cola was a _____ for the Olympic Games in Atlanta.
4. The company _____ that people drink 38 million gallons of Coke worldwide each day.

b As You Watch

1. You will hear some place names in the video. Put a check mark (✓)
next to the ones you hear.

- ☐ a. Cairo (Egypt)
- ☐ b. Eastern Europe
- ☐ c. South America
- ☐ d. Russia
- ☐ e. Middle East
- ☐ f. Central America
- ☐ g. Atlanta (United States)
- ☐ h. China
- ☐ i. Australia
- ☐ j. Africa

2. Did you see these things in the video? Check (✓) Yes or No.

	Yes	No
a. Crates of Coca-Cola with the logo	☐	☐
b. Young people drinking Coke	☐	☐
c. A couple fighting over who gets the last Coke	☐	☐
d. The Coca-Cola script	☐	☐
e. A man walking a dog with the Coke logo behind him	☐	☐
f. An ice-skater spinning on a can of Coke	☐	☐
g. The Coke logo on the cover of a magazine	☐	☐
h. A dog running away with a baby's can of Coke	☐	☐

C | After You Watch

1. Part of the video is about the choice of the city for the 1996 Olympic Games. The two main contestants were Athens, Greece, the home of the first Olympic Games, and Atlanta, United States, the home of Coca-Cola. Below are comments about their cities from a Greek official and a U.S. official. Read the comments, and then write Greek *or* U.S.

_____ official: My city is the home of the Olympics. We played in the first Olympic Games thousands of years ago.

_____ official: My city is the home of Coca-Cola. It has offered millions of dollars if we get the games.

_____ official: My city has lots of money.

_____ official: My city has lots of history.

_____ official: We have stadiums that are thousands of years old.

_____ official: We can build stadiums that cost millions of dollars.

2. Many countries were not happy when Atlanta won. They felt that Coca-Cola bought the Olympic Games to advertise its product. Which side are you on? Do you think that having sponsors for the Olympics is a good idea? Add two more reasons under the side you choose.

For Sponsors: *I think it's great to have sponsors for the Olympic Games. They can help poor athletes buy equipment.*	**Against Sponsors:** *I think sponsors for the Olympic Games are a bad idea. The athletes they help have to advertise the company products.*

Activity Page

Crossword Puzzle

Across

2. We hope scientists find a _____ for cancer.
4. Copy
6. A type of metal
7. Exchanged
10. Rules that govern a society
12. Easy to remember
13. Paper money

Down

1. Customers
2. Smart
3. Not wanting to spend money
4. An unkind action
5. Bad behavior
6. Show
8. Talk about
9. Nearly
11. Picture
13. The person in charge

Capitalization and Abbreviation

Both capitalization and abbreviations are often used in business. Most trademarks (Coca-Cola, Toyota, Kodak) are capitalized, and many are abbreviated (IBM, BP, Aramco).

1. **Capitalization.** Your dictionary shows when a word needs capital letters. Look at the entries below. Circle the entry that is capitalized. In the middle entry, count the number of capital letters that come *after* the words *Usage Note*. Put the number in the circle.

   afraid /əˈfreɪd / *adjective*
   fearful: *The child is afraid of dogs and cries when one comes close.*

   African-American /ˈæfrɪkən/ *noun*
   an American whose ancestors were African: *He is an African-American.* – *adjective* **African-American.** *See*: black.

   Usage Note: Compare *African-American* and *black*. In the United States, the terms *African-American* and *black* are both used to talk about Americans of African descent. Some people use the term *African-American;* others prefer the term *black*. Both are acceptable.

   after /ˈæftər/ *preposition*
   1 in back of, behind: *I told my dog to stay home, but he came after me.*
   2 later in time: *We had dinner after the movie.*

   after *conjunction*
   later than: *She came to the party after I did.* (antonym) before.

2. **Abbreviation.** A shortened, or abbreviated, form of a word or phrase is an abbreviation. Abbreviations do not have to be capitalized. Underline the abbreviations in the dictionary entries below. Which of the underlined entries do you think are the most useful to businesspeople? Circle five or six.

   ad /æd/ *noun informal*
   short for advertisement

   afford /əˈfɔrd/ *verb*
   to be able to do or pay for something: *We can't afford to buy that expensive car; we don't have enough money.*

ASAP or asap
abbreviation of as soon as possible: *Call me ASAP.*

ATM /
abbreviation of automated teller machine

CD /ˌsiˈdi/ *noun*
abbreviation of compact disc: *I bought my favorite singer's new CD today.*

C.O.D. or COD /ˌsioʊˈdi/ *noun*
abbreviation of cash on delivery, meaning that one pays the person who delivers the goods for the goods and for the cost of sending them: *I paid for the shoes C.O.D.*

elsewhere /ˈɛlsˌwɛr/ *adverb*
in some other place: *She doesn't live here; she must live elsewhere.*

ELT /ˌiˌɛlˈti/
abbreviation of English Language Teaching

E-mail or e-mail /ˈiˌmeɪl/ *noun*
short for electronic mail

GNP /ˌdʒiˌɛnˈpi/ *noun*
abbreviation of gross national product

ID or ID card /ˈaɪˈdi/ *noun*
abbreviation of identification card

IOU /ˈaɪoʊˈyu/
abbreviation of I owe you: a written promise to pay back money

IPA /ˈaɪpiˈei/
abbreviation of International Phonetic Alphabet

nearby /ˌnɪrˈbaɪ/ *adverb*
close: *Is there a post office nearby?*

U.N. /ˌyuˈɛn/ *noun*
abbreviation of United Nations

In the space provided, write in the correct abbreviation.

1. He quickly wrote out an _____ for the missing money. (IOU, ASAP, ID)

2. Please give me an answer _____. (GNP, IPA, ASAP)

3. Jenny put an _____ in the newspaper to sell her bicycle. (ad, COD, ID)

4. The _____ of that country rose by 10 percent in two years. (ATM, U.N., GNP)

5. I have no cash. I'll have to go to the _____ after work. (U.N., ATM, ID)

Vocabulary

a

absence 127
accept 10
advertising 172
ahead 54
almost 178
amazingly 65
amount 81
ancient 92
apart 5
appearance 121
aside 49
at least 60
athletes 49
attention 104
avoid 81

b

backs 54
ballpoint pen 15
battle 43
bend 5
besides 81
bills 165
bitter 92
boss 178
bribe 186
bright 139
bury 86

c

cages 98
captured 43
career 65
carpenters 26
cash 178

challenging 186
chemicals 86
circle 54
clever 172
clients 185
cliffs 133
climate 21
clues 121
coach 65
coins 165
committee 60
compared (to) 127
conditions 104
contain 81
contents 178
contests 60
contrast 179
controls 172
court 172
covered 139
crater 133
credit 193
crew 121
critics 98
crossed 10
cubic 26
cultures 185
cure 172
currency 165
curse 121
customers 81
customs 185
cycle 146

d

dairy 86
damage 121
debt 194
decided 26
decreasing 98
defeating 43

delicious 86
delivered 10
descendants 128
deserted 121
dessert 92
diary 121
dip 15
direction 178
disappeared 127
discovered 92
discuss 186
distance 26
double 81
dozens 5
dropped 178

e

eager 127
elbows 43
eliminating 60
embarrassing 5
encouraged 65
engineer 5
equator 26
events 60
eventually 98
excellent 54
except 49
experiences 86
experimenting 98
explanations 121
explosion 139
extinct 98

f

factory 178
facts 166
familiar 86

fascinating 166
fastened 5
favorite 92
fight 127
fill 15
flat 139
fold up 21
forbids 86
foreign 86
found out 86
fountain pen 15
freedom 43
frequently 65
function 104

g

generation 145
gesture 185
giants 133
gloves 43
glue 10
graphite 15
grind 15
ground 139

h

hit 43
hold 15
hooks 5
hostile 127
huge 121
humans 98

i

identical 128
illnesses 104

209

image 172
imagine 145
imitate 172
immediately 10
in addition 139
in full 193
inconvenient 165
independence 104
indicate 165
indigestion 104
individual 54
inflation 179
ingredient 92
inhabitants 133
injustice 104
ink 15
inspect 121
insult 185
interest 194
involved 194
iron 165
isolated 133
issued 193

 j

journey 145

 k

kick 43
kneel 43

 l

laws 186
lead 15
leaked 15
length 26
lined up 178
loaded 178
locations 133
logo 172

 m

mail 10
market 172
mass marketing 172
match 43
measure 26
medal 65
members 10
memorable 172
metal 165
meteor 139
methods 98
metric system 26
miss 81
misunderstandings 185
multipurpose 193
mystery 121

 n

national 49
normal 81

 o

object 21
occasions 104
odd 127
offered 194
offspring 146
on purpose 81
once 92
oppose 60
order 86
overcome 65
owners 193

 p

participated 60
plan 54
plateau 139

points 15
political 104
population 98
postage stamp 10
pour 92
powerful 81
pray 43
precious 165
prepaid 10
present 133
prevent 133
princes 21
princess 21
processed 98
profitable 194
protest 104
proud 43

 q

quite a few 65

 r

rapidly 98
rare 86
realized 133
receipts 165
received 10
recent 60
reflect 60
relationships 185
remove 60
reported 139
reproduces 145
rest 43
retired 65
revolution 26
ring 49
risk 81
rolled 133
row 5
royalty 21
rude 185

run 54
rushes 49

 s

sank 121
scary 86
seems 21
series 49
serious 65
settled 127
shape 15
shook 139
shortage 98
similar 54
site 139
slides 5
snack 92
so far 140
solemn 133
solid 92
solved 5
statues 133
steps 49
stingy 186
strips 5
strong 49
suggested 139
survived 179

t

tags 145
term 86
theory 133
throw 54
tiny 145
took place 60
took turns 65
touches 49
tournaments 49
tracked 145
traded 165
training 49
treatments 65
tribes 21

unique 172

valleys 54
valued 92

vanished 128
violence 121
volunteers 146
vote 104

war 127
wealthy 92

weapons 43
whatever 15
wherever 54
willing 172
wondered
    145
worry 98
worth 165
wouldn't 21

yet 81

zipper 5

Skills Index

ACTIVITY PAGE
Crossword puzzles, 37, 206
Guessing sports, 74
Newspaper headlines, 157
Restaurants, 114
Sporting needs, 74
Verbs, 158

DICTIONARY PAGE
Abbreviation, 207–208
Antonyms, 38
Capitalization, 207
Informal usage, 159–160
Parts of speech, 115–116
Phonetic spelling, 76
Pronunciation, 75–76
Stress, 75

READING
Comprehension, 7–8, 12–13, 18, 23–24, 28–29,
    46, 51–52, 57, 63, 67–68, 84, 89–90, 95–96,
    101–102, 107, 124–125, 130–131, 136–137,
    142–143, 148–149, 168–169, 175–176, 182,
    189–190, 196
Context clues, 2–3, 40–41, 78–79, 118–119,
    162–163
Main ideas, 8, 13, 19, 24, 30, 47, 52, 58, 63, 68, 84,
    90, 96, 102, 107, 125, 131, 137, 143, 149, 170,
    176, 183, 191, 197
Pre-reading activities, 4, 9, 14, 20, 25, 42, 48, 53,
    59, 64, 80, 85, 91, 97, 103, 120, 126, 132, 138,
    144, 164, 171, 177, 184, 192
Vocabulary, 6–7, 11–12, 16–17, 22–23, 27–28,
    44–45, 50–51, 55–57, 61–62, 66–67, 82–83,
    87–89, 93–95, 99–101, 105–106, 122–124,
    128–130, 134–136, 140–142, 146–148,
    166–168, 173–175, 180–181, 186–189,
    194–196

SPEAKING
Ordering meals, 114
Partner activities, 74, 114

TEST-TAKING SKILLS
Checking off choices, 35, 73, 160, 204
Classification, 116, 205
Fill in blanks, 6–7, 11–12, 16–17, 22–23, 27–28,
    33, 38, 44–45, 50–51, 55–57, 61–62, 66–67,
    70–71, 72, 82–83, 87–88, 93–95, 99–100,
    105–106, 109, 110, 111, 112, 115, 122–124,
    128–129, 134–135, 140–141, 146–148, 150,
    152, 155, 166–168, 173–174, 180–181,
    186–188, 194–195, 198, 199, 200–201, 202,
    203, 208
Matching, 23, 30, 45, 51, 67, 69, 76, 89, 101, 113,
    130, 136, 153, 175, 189
Multiple-choice questions, 2–3, 7–8, 18, 23–24,
    40–41, 46, 51–52, 63, 67–68, 76, 78–79,
    89–90, 101–102, 118–119, 124–125, 130–131,
    142–143, 159, 162–163, 168–169, 175–176,
    189–190
Sentence completion, 38, 108, 111, 198–199
Sequencing items, 182
Short-answer questions, 8, 13, 19, 24, 29, 46–47,
    52, 58, 63, 68, 84, 90, 96, 102, 107, 113, 125,
    131, 137, 143, 149, 170, 176, 182, 190–191,
    197
True/false questions, 12–13, 28–29, 36, 57, 84,
    95–96, 107, 112, 136–137, 148–149, 155, 196
Underlining words that do not belong, 62, 106,
    142, 196

TOPICS
Business, 161–197
    Global business, 184–191
    History of money, 164–170
    Inflation, 177–183
    Mass marketing, 171–176
    Plastic money, 192–197
Food, 78–107
    Blue revolution, 97–102
    Chocolate, 91–96
    Foods from around the world, 85–90
    Puffer fish, 80–84
    Twenty-one days without food, 103–107
Inventions and inventors, 1–30
    Metric system, 25–30
    Pencils and pens, 14–19
    Postage stamp, 9–13
    Umbrella, 20–24
    Zipper, 4–8
Mysteries, 117–149
    Easter Island statues, 132–137
    Marie Celeste, 120–125
    Monarch butterflies, 144–149
    Roanoke settlement, 126–131
    Tunguska fireball, 138–143

Sports, 39–68
    Great athletes, 64–68
    Olympic sports, 59–63
    Sumo wrestling, 48–52
    Tarahumara foot races, 53–58
    Thai boxing, 42–47

VIEWING
Video highlights, 35–36, 72–73, 112–113,
    155–156, 203–205

WORD STUDY
Adjectives
    With *-able*, 109
    With *-ive*, 199
Collocations, 111, 153, 202
Compound words, 69
Conjunctions, 150
how + adjective, 32
Map study, 69
Nouns
    Count/noncount nouns, 108
    Plural forms, 151
Spelling, 151
Suffixes
    Adjectives with *-able*, 109
    Adjectives with *-ive*, 199

Verbs
    Future tense, 31
    Gerunds, 198–199
    Irregular verbs, 32, 71, 153
    Past tense, 32, 71, 111, 153, 201
    Regular verbs, 153
    will or *be + going to*, 31
Word forms, 33, 70–71, 110, 152, 200–201
Writing short answers, 34, 71, 111, 154, 202

WRITING
Arguments, 205
Charts, 35
Crossword puzzles, 37, 206
Maps, 156
Newspaper headlines, 157
Partner activities, 158
Sentences, 31, 32, 74, 109, 153
Short answers, 8, 13, 19, 24, 34, 46–47, 52, 58, 63,
    68, 71, 84, 90, 96, 102, 107, 111, 113, 125,
    131, 137, 143, 149, 154, 170, 176, 182,
    190–191, 197, 202

Irregular Verbs

Simple	Past	Simple	Past
be	was, were	hold	held
become	became	hurt	hurt
begin	began	keep	kept
blow	blew	know	knew
bring	brought	lead	led
build	built	leave	left
buy	bought	lose	lost
catch	caught	make	made
choose	chose	meet	met
come	came	pay	paid
cut	cut	put	put
do (does)	did	ring	rang
drink	drank	run	ran
drive	drove	see	saw
eat	ate	sell	sold
fall	fell	send	sent
feel	felt	sleep	slept
fight	fought	slide	slid
find	found	speak	spoke
fly	flew	spend	spent
forget	forgot	sweep	swept
freeze	froze	take	took
get	got	teach	taught
give	gave	tell	told
go (goes)	went	think	thought
grow	grew	understand	understood
have (has)	had	wear	wore
hear	heard	win	won
hit	hit	write	wrote

214